The Trial of Luther

HISTORIC TRIALS SERIES
Editor: J. P. Kenyon, Professor of History, University of Hull

The Trial of Luther

James Atkinson

𝔖𝔇 Stein and Day / *Publishers* / New York

First published in the United States of America
by Stein and Day/*Publishers* 1971
Copyright © James Atkinson 1971

Library of Congress Catalog Card No. 72–104626
All rights reserved
Printed in Great Britain by Willmer Brothers Limited, Birkenhead,
Cheshire and bound by C. Tinling and Co. Ltd. Prescot, Lancs.
for Stein and Day/*Publishers*/ 7 East 48 Street, New York, N.Y. 10017

SBN 8128–1361–8

Contents

Illustrations

ACKNOWLEDGEMENT

The Author and Publishers wish to thank the following for permission to reproduce the illustrations in this book: The Abington Press for fig. 5 (from Bainton, *Here I Stand*); the Bibliothèque Municipale, Arras and Photographie Giraudon for fig. 9; the Trustees of the British Museum for figs. 2, 3, 6 and 10; the Budapest Museum of Fine Arts for fig. 12; the Mansell Collection for figs. 7 and 8.

Sources and Abbreviations

WA D. *Martin Luthers Werke. Kritische Gesamtausgabe.* Weimar 1883– . Contains books, commentaries, disputations, sermons etc. References to volume, page, line.

WABr D. *Martin Luthers Werke. Briefwechsel.* Weimar 1930– . Correspondence. Reference to number of letter, or page and line.

WADB D. *Martin Luthers Werke. Deutsche Bibel.* Weimar 1906–61 (Luther's Bible translation.)

WATi D. *Martin Luthers Werke. Tischreden.* Weimar 1912–21. Table Talk. Reference to number of piece.

RA *Deutsche Reichstagsakten.* Jungere Reihe. II Band. Gotha 1896 (repr. Göttinger 1962). Reference to volume, page, line.

Luther's Works, gen. edd. Pelikan and Lehmann (1955–). American Edition.

Corpus Juris Canonici, ed. Aemilius Friedberg. Leipzig 1881.

Bullarium. Turin 1857–85. There are many bullaria, notably that of Cherubini 1586, Luxembourg 1727–30, Mainardi 1733–62, but the nineteenth-century Turin edition is more generally available and easier to consult.

Denzinger, H. *Enchiridion Symbolorum.* 30th Edition (ed. Karl Rahner) Freiburg 1955.

Gee, Henry and Hardy, William J. *Documents illustrative of English Church History.* London 1896.

Kidd, B. J. *Documents illustrative of the Continental Reformation.* Oxford 1911.

Table of Chronology

	Judica	*Palm Sunday*	*Easter*	*Quasi-modo-geneti*	*Misere-cordias Domine*	*Jubilate*	*Cantate*
Sunday	17	24	31	7	14	21	28
Monday	18	25	1	8	15	22	29
Tuesday	19	26	2	9	16	23	30
Wednesday	20	27	3	10	17	24	
Thursday	21	28	4	11	18	25	
Friday	22	*Good Friday* 29	5	12	19	26	
Saturday	23	30	6	13	20	27	

1 First Hearing: Before Cardinal Cajetan at the Diet of Augsburg

12–14 October 1518

Luther—the man and the crisis

'Luther at Worms is the most pregnant and momentous fact in our history...' wrote Lord Acton. Contemporary and subsequent historians have made similar judgments. They have been quick to see that when Luther held his ground before papacy and empire, when he refused to betray his conscience, his spiritual scruples and his academic principles, a deliverance was effected, a tyranny broken. In that dramatic stand at Worms in 1521, immortalized by those humble but memorable words, 'Here I stand! I can no other!', Luther secured for posterity both academic and spiritual liberty. He broke the quasi-infallible authority of the Church over the university as well as the stultifying hold of the clergy over the laity, thereby liberating the minds, souls and consciences of his contemporaries, intellectual and non-intellectual alike. The old medieval world died and our modern era was born when Luther burnt the papal bull at Wittenberg in December 1520 and faced his charges at Worms four months later in April 1521.

The charges against Luther were, in short, heresy and disobedience. They had been formulated in various ways at different times in sundry briefs, bulls and debates over a period of four years, 1517–21, at the end of which Luther was excommunicated and outlawed. Luther's defence and explanation of his position lasted not only throughout these four years but till his death twenty-five years later in 1546. Nevertheless, for the purpose of this enquiry his defence will be confined to these same four years, and will comprise Luther's defence as found in disputations, letters and books, as well as his defence at his first hearing (Augsburg 1518), his defence in official disputation (Leipzig 1519) and finally his defence at Worms 1521.

Before assessing the debate a few preliminary considerations may not inappropriately be borne in mind. First, the debate since its closure at Worms has been bedevilled by controversy and perverted by partisanship. Here the *odium theologicum* has been at its worst. For over 400 years Catholicism has anathematized Luther, and for the same period Protestantism (with most secular and liberal historians), has been favourable. Yet the debate did not begin in this atmosphere: nor does the atmosphere help us to judge it. In his early years as a monk Luther had been a model of propriety when as a Doctor of Theology he had sought to debate the theology associated with indulgences. It was only when the Curia sought to silence him unheard that he refused to be so silenced. It was at that moment of his first hearing before Cajetan at Augsburg in 1518, when Staupitz, his spiritual superior, who had previously shown Luther much affection and esteem, and who had appointed Luther to the chair at Wittenberg which he himself had just vacated, and who had come to Augsburg to support Luther, finally realized that Luther would stand and what Luther's stand would mean. Staupitz combed Augsburg to raise funds to get Luther out of the country to save him and thereby prevent the dispute coming to a head. He failed in this plan, so unilaterally hurriedly released Luther from his vow of obedience as an Augustinian monk, and fled from Augsburg to leave Luther to his fate. From that moment on, though Luther continued to wear his habit many years longer, he was not a monk under obedience but rather a lone Catholic scholar occupying a chair of theology at Wittenberg. It was at that moment, when Staupitz discharged Luther from his vow of obedience, that Protestantism was born, though the word came into existence only some twelve years later at the Diet of Speier 1529. From that same moment Catholicism had to bear from within the gradual weakening of its authority and the growing questioning of its theology. The reader with religious views may find it as hard to estimate the evidence as the reader with none, though for different reasons. In either case he must beware of the *odium theologicum* and come to the evidence unbiassed, as a good jury man.

The second point to bear in mind is related. It is not only important to free the mind of theological prejudice and passion, it is equally essential to realize that the entire matter is nevertheless theological through and through, and for its just appraisement demands theological judgements. In the sixteenth century the theological issues involved split Europe into two, and caught up the entire community in the turmoil, but today only a minority can grasp the issues at all. Yet it still remains true that Luther's sole concern was about God: he was simply a theologian. He wanted men to know God: to know the God who was reconciling man to himself in Christ, that all men, prince and pauper, priest and peasant, may alike learn pardon for their sin and the 'peace which passeth all understanding'. In our critical, contemporary, agnostic and secularized climate of opinion this may appear to the reader utterly *demodé,* though that in itself does not make the statement any less true. Not to grant that Luther's sole concern was God, in fact not to understand this concern, however unpalatable or unacceptable or incomprehensible, will ensure a failure to understand Luther at Worms.

Many an otherwise reputable historian tenders an interpretation of Luther's protest on the evidence (perfectly true as far as it goes) of social, political or economic concerns by simply cutting the Gordian knot of theology. They adopt the practical hardheaded policy of a Pilate who, in judging Christ, settled the matter by criteria he understood, and washed his hands before the court of the real theological issue at stake. Or of a Gallio, who in judging Paul under a similar condemnation 'cared for none of these things'. It is a matter of verifiable historical fact that many of Luther's contemporaries, Catholic and Protestant alike, baulked this issue, too. Consequently, they used Luther's protest and power to further in that climate of unrest their own ends, and thereby muddied the stream in directing it through their own backyards.

This blunt opinion must be justified. For instance, realizing their traditional role was at an end in the new society, the knights and lesser nobility lined up with the Reformation against the Pope and against the emperor; the peasants capitalized Luther's radical and reformatory social thinking in support of their cause; the humanists were strengthened in their cause of intellectual freedom when Luther dispelled scholastic obscurantism from within. Yet Luther was not on the side of the knights, at all, nor of the peasants, nor of the humanists. Von Sickingen and Hutten, Erasmus and Münzer knew this at the time. Luther no more let the peasants down than he let the nobility or the humanists down. To varying extents they all turned against Luther when they realized that they did not have his unqualified party support. He was engaged on another battle, the battle for theological truth, and would not be led aside to fight any other causes, even just ones.

If then it be conceded that Luther's sole concern was God (or at the least granted as a working hypothesis to understand Luther in his sixteenth-century situation), the reader not only estimates the contemporary arguments more sensitively, but is further delivered from all those simplified pictures of Luther derived from alien presuppositions of the nineteenth and twentieth centuries. He will see Luther for what he was, a theologian and religious reformer; not the great champion of individual liberty and private judgment, not the rugged peasant who challenged Pope and emperor, not the Germanic Hercules, not the social emancipator, not the angry young man struggling with a father complex and an identity crisis nor any other of these historical recreations, prompted by religious, social, intellectual, even psychoanalytical interests, alien to the sixteenth-century Luther. Luther was a theologian of the sixteenth century, educated in the dying world of scholasticism, caught up in an upsurge of humanist enlightenment and cataclysmic social and political change, but a man with the single and simple motivation of restoring his Church and world to God in Christ. No more, but no less.

The Reformation was no sudden event. We all now start from the experience of a Christendom divided, but we have constantly to remind ourselves that the process of division took years. Not only did the debate last a long time, but as late as twenty years after Worms at the Diet of Regensburg 1541 Rome and the Protestants had reached agreement again, even on the divisive article of justification by faith. Admittedly, Luther had been excluded from the Diet for he was under the ban, but under the able and eirenic leadership of Melanchthon, terms of unity had been actually agreed. It was only when Cardinal Contarini took the terms to Rome that the papal curia rejected them owing to a changed political and religious climate. The same process took much longer in England, where it was not till as late as 1570 that Pope Pius V finally excommunicated Elizabeth and freed 'his subjects' from their allegiance to the English crown. However these facts be interpreted, it is certainly clear that Protestantism was an open debatable position for close on fifty years. Non-sectarian Protestants would aver that there is still a debate to be finished : some of the best contemporary Roman Catholic scholars show their inclination to resume the debate. It is not unimportant to view the debate as still in process.

The Reformation was a real re-formation, a re-orientation of a thousand years of Christian living and thinking. Martin Luther, in fact, was an exemplary representation of the medieval establishment, yet he did more than any other single person to demolish it by seeking to re-form it according to its own principles and pretensions. He was a critical conservative. He sought not to change but to conserve: to open men's minds to what they already had, to what they had long lost.

What kind of man was he then? Why did this professor from the academic Nazareth of Europe succeed where so many distinguished predecessors had failed? How did this man catch at the flood the tide in the affairs of men? Why was it that over the centuries Rome had crushed every previous reformer, yet could not crush this man, whose success fathered a generation of such men throughout the universities of Europe? Who, looking at the map of Europe in 1517, peopled by men of the distinction of Erasmus, Colet and More; Michelangelo, Leonardo da Vinci, Raphael and Titian; Henry VIII, Francis I, and Charles V; and the host of intellectual, cultural and political leaders, explorers, thinkers and scholars of the day, would have put his finger on the University of Wittenberg and knocked at the door of Professor Luther in the Black Cloister to say, 'Here is where it will all start! This is the man who will do it!' Luther himself would not have believed it. In fact a year earlier when an academic 'Who's Who' of Europe was compiled, Martin Luther was not mentioned.

Born of hard-working, God-fearing parents in the little town of Eisleben, Saxony on 10 November 1483—the lovely house, still lived in, stands there to this day with its secluded garden and its fine old gate in a quiet cobbled street—Martin Luther enjoyed a privileged childhood. At school he quickly learned to read and write, and gained an uncommon mastery both of music and Latin, in the company of sons of professional men. In 1501, when Luther was eighteen, his father sent him, at his own cost, to Germany's ancient and most famous university of Erfurt, where he studied Law with distinction, and as early as 1505 had acquired both his BA and MA degrees.

It was a very disturbed and exciting time when Luther was growing up. Those were the days of the great discoverers and voyagers when Columbus and Cabot talked of the new worlds they had discovered. When Copernicus was trying to convince the world that the sun was the centre of the universe not the world. When the microscope and telescope were invented to show the microcosm and the macrocosm. When Renaissance scholars were stimulating thought in Europe with the rediscovery of Hellenism, and artists of genius were beautifying their splendid edifices. The political scene was a time of violent, almost cataclysmic upsurge. Europe was preparing to elect a new emperor and was about to enter a long series of world wars. Suleiman II was advancing ominously and when the single-minded Turk towered over Europe, Christendom itself was divided, with France and Germany at daggers drawn. Not only was Charles V engaged in a desperate contest with Francis I, but the estates of Germany consisting of princes, high ecclesiastics and free cities were seeking more independence from the Emperor as well as relief from papal taxation. The Papacy and the Curia were also heavily embroiled in sordid political intrigue and power politics. Feudalism was marching with Marxist inevitability into capitalism. Currency rather than goods was taking pre-eminence in trade. The great banking houses had arisen, as well as trading companies, monopolies and all the machinery of capitalism. Victimized country peasant and down-trodden urbanized proletariat alike craved for a new deal of justice, decency and freedom, for they were all desperately short of money.

The young man Luther was in the vortex of all these disturbances as well as the inner conflicts of what to make of his life and career, and in order to find peace of mind and a life with God, he turned his back on the world and became a monk, joining the prestigious monastery of the Augustinians in Erfurt on 17 July 1505.

In the monastery Luther was not to work in silence for the perfection of his soul, but was singled out by his superiors to resume studies in the school of the monastery. His studies spoke to his condition. Here he met the same problems which were besetting his own mind: the problem of grace and merit, of sin, of free will, of election and predestination. Luther began to form the view that the accepted answers were unsatisfactory and grew markedly disquieted, and found himself almost obsessed by his theological problems. His mentors and fellow monks noticed the deep intellectual perturbation of the young monk but marked at the same time his profound piety.

It is not the theme of this book to discuss the scholasticism in which Luther was educated except to indicate its essential nature which caused Luther to oppose it, even destroy it, and which eventually brought him to his trial. The Renaissance scholars made merciless fun of it, but Luther opposed it from within not only on intellectual grounds but on spiritual and theological grounds. Whereas the Renaissance scholars laughed, Luther wept at its demise.

A great deal of research is going on in the field of scholasticism, and at the moment it is difficult to arrive at settled judgments. The reader should not uncritically accept the all too common historical text book caricature of late medieval thinking as wasting the understanding and intellect in dry formalism and subtle but barren controversies, without casting his mind back on its not ignoble one thousand years of learning. Most modern historians deal with scholasticism in the hour of its decay, when, rendered ineffective by foolish party strife between the schools, it fell between the pincer thrusts of the Renaissance and the Reformation. Modern man, therefore, tends to approach it in a critical almost a rebellious frame of mind, yet at its best it was a creditable attempt both to understand Christianity and to integrate it with current intellectual movements. It was a method of philosophical and theological speculation rigorously controlled by fine logical analysis. Scholasticism had sought successfully for a whole millenium to penetrate the meaning of revealed Christian truth by definition, analogy, logic and dialectic, and by means of these processes to systematize that knowledge.

The intellectual life of early Christianity had been centred in Athens, Alexandria, Antioch and Carthage. In medieval Christendom the centres moved northwards to the courts of Theodoric and Charlemagne, to Paris and Cologne, to Canterbury and Oxford. This shift meant that medieval Christendom had to acquire a language, a culture, a philosophy, a theology quite new to its traditions, and in addition master the patristic corpus of the East. That whole scholarly activity of the schools was what we now call scholasticism, in other words, a prolonged system of schooling ('Schoolasticism', if one may be allowed to coin such a word). It was a long process of learning: an ordering and an assimilation by the Frankish–Nordic mind of that immense and alien corpus. The tragedy of scholasticism was that at the end of one thousand years of this remarkable process the new developing world of science demanded a learning attitude that would not merely conserve and re-express old knowledge, but an attitude that could assimilate fresh empirical evidence. When the learning attitude of scholasticism which had been its strength and glory for a thousand years ceased to be its vital concern, scholasticism failed. Grabmann argues an internal decay; Gilson sees it as a matter of intellectual confusion and disorder; de Wulf as a lack of minds, not of ideas.

However we understand the causes, there is no doubt of its failure. It was this failure of a system that had endured for a thousand years which was one factor which made men's minds the more ready to hear the reformers. It is a matter of historic fact that Luther's attack on Catholicism began not with the indulgences controversy of 1517 but with a corroding criticism of scholasticism some five years earlier. As early as 1512–13 there can be clearly discerned Luther's criticism of scholasticism in the lectures on the Bible which he gave at Wittenberg when he was appointed to the Chair of the Bible. Certainly by 1515 in his lectures on Romans there is sustained and scholarly criticism

B

which culminated in an open *Disputation against the Scholastic Theology* in 1517, before the indulgences controversy.*

The dominating mind in the scholastic tradition was Augustine (354–430). Augustine had had a deep religious experience, and when his massive intellect expressed his powerful Pauline evangelical theology in incisive, poetical and paradoxical language within a Platonic framework, he gave Christendom the basis for a rational belief in God as well as a biblical view of fallen man in need of grace.

It is a paradox that the strength of scholasticism was its rationalism, and yet it was its rapier-like rationalism which destroyed it from within. The saving antidote which had neutralized the acids of its own rationalism in the early centuries had been its mysticism, which had served to keep a balance for some centuries owing to the work of Pseudo-Dionysius and Erigena (c. 810–c.877). Anselm of Canterbury (c.1033–c.1109) was opposed to this kind of approach and sought to establish an imposing defence of Christianity on the sole basis of reason without recourse to an appeal either to tradition or scripture. Abailard (1079–1142) maintained this powerful strain of a rationalist logical technique, and opened up the debate between realism and nominalism which lasted to Luther's day. (The realist thought of reality in terms of ideas or universals. The nominalist argued that ideas, e.g. 'power', or universals, e.g. 'rose', do not in fact exist at all. The words are just names which are useful for logical thinking, all we in fact know are examples of power or instances of roses.)

This debate liberated scholasticism from its Platonism (very good to express theology), to a new Aristotelianism (essential to relate theology to the new, empirical, scientific thinking). It was Thomas Aquinas (1226–74) who made a brilliant synthesis of revelation and reason. He combined an Aristotelian realism with a powerful Augustinian theology of God, sin, predestination

* For a full translation of this document with commentary see James Atkinson, *Library of Christian Classics*, Vol. XVI, pp. 251–73.

and grace. He sought to vindicate Christianity at the bar of reason, and to answer any and every objection to it. He argued two sources of knowledge of God—creation and revelation. Creation was to be explored and examined: revelation could only be accepted, shown to be reasonable, and finally related to other knowledge by analogy.

Luther between 1513–16 had grown to oppose Thomism. He deplored its loss of the Augustinian emphases on sin and grace, its teaching of merit, its 'pagan ethics' (Luther's phrase), its teaching on the free will, its semi-Pelagianism (man can effect his own better relationship to God), its non-biblical doctrine of transubstantiation, and its papalism. Already we discern the reformer in the young Professor Luther.

Two British monks had been far severer critics of Thomas, Duns Scotus (c.1264–c.1308) and William of Ockham (1300–49). The former opposed any thinking which sought to express God in terms of mind and concepts, who he taught could be understood only in terms of will and act. Ockham, famous for his 'razor' which he used to cut out the hypostasisation of terms, taught that man could know nothing of God apart from revelation. More than any other man Ockham dissolved scholasticism.

A strange mood of melancholic uncertainty began to pervade Europe when the theologians themselves were exercising solvent, even destructive, tendencies. Luther's university teachers were Ockhamists, and he imbibed all this thinking—until he himself overthrew it. We cannot here assess the influence of Ockham on Luther. Suffice it to say when Luther achieved full theological stature as a professor of theology, men were already tired of scholasticism. Scholars found its deductive reasoning unacceptable because they could not accept the premises with which the schoolmen started. The schoolmen failed to meet the intellectual demands of their own day. Natural science was born and metaphysics died: the old learning was flouted, ridiculed, and overthrown by humanism and its empirical method. The age of logic and speculation was past. The battles of the Reformation were to be fought over questions of fact and truth examined by linguistic and historical analysis, whether it was a passage of scripture or a point of doctrine. Theology could no longer be considered a vast corpus of dogma infallibly deduced from elementary data outside the range of normal critical principles. Luther and his contemporaries examined the data. Was it true? Did it answer to the facts of experience and was it examinable by normal processes of mind and by normal critical criteria? The reformers with their contemporaries raised these questions— and found satisfying answers. The scholastics could put up no fight. They were pedants who had lost the ear of the people and the regard of the scholar. They returned to their own privacies and died off. But, though the humanists' onslaught on Scholasticism was devastating, Luther went one stage further. He laid bare its inadequacies not only for the scholar but for the common man to see, and provided in its place a biblical theology which liberated mankind from scholastic sophistries to the empirical, verifiable biblical account of what God had done and said. This at once secularized Christian theology and ethics making them relevant to ordinary everyday life and verifiable in the light of one's own experience and thinking. This was a vital shift in authority. Truth was no longer an authoritative declaration *de haut en bas,* rather perception by an awakened individual.

Luther had been right through the whole course of scholasticism as well as the long discipline of monasticism. He knew at first hand that the scholastic theology could not talk about God with authority, conviction or truth, and that the monastic discipline could not get a man in touch with God. He knew at first hand that the theology of the day was erroneous; he knew at first hand that the religious practices of his day got nobody anywhere. He wrestled for years with a false theology and a mistaken practice, until he found a true theology and a true practice, against a false faith in the interests of true faith. He found the errors, and discerned thereby the truths. He really fought the Papal Church in the interests of the Church, and sought not to destroy its authority but to re-establish it on the sounder basis of the Bible, reason and sound tradition. He sought to provide thinking reasonable men with better answers than those they were given. Some of his work is polemical, not only because he was attacked and fought back, but because a large part of his work was the demolition of accretions and innovations that had blinded men for centuries—papal infallibility and transubstantiation; saint worship and the centrality of Mary rather than Christ; pilgrimages, shrines, wonder-working images, holy water, meritorious works and all near-pagan Catholic folk lore and popular cultus; paid masses for the dead, indulgences and purgatory. The Papal Curia resisted Luther, and consequently polemical writings and disputations arose. In these verbal battles the great watchwords of the Reformation were sparked off, e.g. 'the Word of God', 'faith alone', 'priesthood of all believers', 'justification by faith alone' and the like. These war cries were essentially rallying cries to preserve truths of Christianity under threat of disappearing before the omnivorous claims of papal infallibility. The catchwords have no intrinsic value and express no new truth. They were undefeated attempts to maintain the fullness of biblical theology against the Curia which denied it. They summarized the old biblical and pre-papalist theology of the ancient church not in novel terms but in the incontrovertible language of their common origins. Luther's debate with Rome was primarily and essentially an attack on scholasticism: not against the Pope, not against abuses and superstitions, not against Catholicism. Catholicism can exist without its popular cultus, and Luther had no objection to the primacy of the Holy Father (provided he was both). It is important to see through the externalities of Luther's trial to the real issues involved. For this reason the reader will meet a lot of Luther's theological argument before he reaches the final trial of a mere two days' debate.

The reformation of the Church had been attempted before Luther in various ways. The movement called Conciliar Reform was a long continued effort to compel the Curia to govern the Church by general council rather than papal fiat. It originated with the learned French canonists of the twelfth century and reached its peak in the fifteenth century. Yet the movement failed ignominiously and the papacy emerged from the conflict stronger than ever.

Deeply religious men had striven for centuries to reform the Church. As early as the twelfth and thirteenth centuries there were movements in France, Germany and Italy: the Albigensians, the Cathari, Francis and the Franciscans. Later there were Wycliffe and the Lollards in England; Huss and the Hussites in Bohemia; John von Goch, John von Wesel, and Johann Wessel in Germany and the Netherlands; Savonarola in Italy; the pious mystics, the Friends of God, the Brethren of the Common Life, all served to make the Church more aware of her de-Christianized secularism and to re-kindle the dying embers. None succeeded, but yet all served to some extent to prepare the way for the new era of Christianity about to dawn.

The Christian Humanists had made their noble attempt: they sought a high morality with an effective church discipline, the machinery of which already existed. They longed for a Christianity simpler and purer, and sought to de-theologise the Church of its scholastic theology. Erasmus, a deeply sincere and believing man, poured scorn on the foibles and fables of established religion, and denounced the Church for its paganism and Judaism. Colet, equally sincere and believing, did the same from the pulpit of St Paul's, London. Yet, for all their brilliance and sincerity the humanists never succeeded in igniting the dying embers. All this was the good side of Christendom in the centuries preceding Luther.

The dark side in the fifteenth and early sixteenth century was very black indeed.

The papacy was utterly secularized. After the scandal of the papal schism was resolved, a slight improvement was discernible, to sink back into the worse corruption of the Borgia popes and their scandalous courts. As was the head so was the body. Many cardinals and priests followed the examples of these depraved popes. Contemporary scholars and satirists are eloquent of the ignorance and immorality of priests and monks. Bishoprics were bought by princes without intellectual or spiritual qualification. Pluralism and absenteeism were rife. Luther's Archbishop, though under age, held three bishoprics and actually bought that of Mainz. Cardinal Wolsey, while Archbishop of York, was chancellor of England, received stipends from France, Italy and Spain, and kept a household of five hundred servants while seeking good preferment for his illegitimate family.

Entire monastic communities had degenerated into hot-beds of superstition and ignorance, idleness and dissipation and were the objects of contempt and ridicule. They had tolled their own death knell in every country of Europe, even if there had been no Reformation.

Theology was not concerned with the Gospel or the Bible, nor with the life of the common man, but had developed into scholastic subtleties, idle speculations and Aristotelian dialectics. It was as far removed from the cause of God as it was from the needs of the people. Brilliant answers were offered to equally dazzling questions, but they were questions spun out of their own mind, questions which nobody asked, the answers to which were utterly irrelevant. Given over to barren logic they petered out in technical argumentation. No less a sympathetic person than the kindly Thomas More said that it was as profitable to read the schoolmen as to milk a billy goat into a sieve.

The Church's worship centred on the Mass, and the priest's duty and power were to effect the miracle of transubstantiation, and to offer the sacrifice for the living and the dead. There was little preaching, for the clergy had nothing to say except on the subject of alms, indulgences, pilgrimages and processions. The churches were full of dubious images and fictitious relics, and other bric à brac many of them allegedly wonder working. Much of this could not escape the condemnation of being idolatrous and of being a barrier against the true God.

Piety, which is essentially an awareness of God issuing in a changed character, had turned outward into an external observance of performances of beads, Paternosters and Ave Marias, fasting, almsgiving, confession to a priest, pilgrimages to a shrine. Good works were religious observances, tainted with the word meritorious. Remission of sin could be bought. Indulgences brazenly hawked around. Any historian knows that the picture is blacker than has been painted, and convention and good manners restrain the pen if not the mind.

There were these two sides. The dark side is attested both by contemporary scholars and now freely admitted by Roman Catholic historians. Within a year of the Diet of Worms, the new Pope, Adrian VI, a man of acknowledged and exceptional integrity, when speaking of enforcing the Edict of Worms against Luther at the Diet of Nurnberg, 1522, gave away his case by decrying the scandals of the Church in Luther's own words: 'From the head corruption has passed to the limbs, from the Pope to the prelates. We have all departed; there is none that doeth good, no, not one.' He described the rising Protestantism as the punishment meeted out to a wicked Catholicism, and promised to remedy the evil, starting with the Curia. The task proved too great for the man. He died within a year (rumour has it of poison). Rome rejoiced at his timely departure and saw to it that his successor, Clement VII, would have no more of that nonsense. When it was called in 1545 the Council of Trent effected a great change certainly, not only theologically but morally, but it was too late to prevent the Protestant schism: the Reformers were not even invited to the Council, and Luther died the following year. The Catholic rump was restored intellectually, morally and spiritually by the Counter-Reformation. True, Catholicism has not seriously lapsed since those days, but her restorers served to make the Catholic Church Roman rather than Catholic and to emphasize its institutionalism, its authoritarianism, its pretensions to infallibility, vices Luther had sought to remove. Trent served the Catholic Church well, but served to harden and worsen the situation in relation to the Reformation.

It is an interesting and fruitful question to ask why it was that when the Church was in an equally sorry plight in the tenth, eleventh and fourteenth centuries, on every occasion she was reformed from within without schism, yet in the sixteenth century she fell apart. Why in the sixteenth century, not earlier? The question is important to understand Luther's trial. The reason suggested is that in the sixteenth century, in the critical hour, Rome resisted reform with all her might, and forced the issue: either no reformation at all, or a reformation with the opposition of Rome. The men who preferred truth to unity were forced out, and forced apart. Rome sought only to condemn Luther and to silence him: she never answered him, she anathematized him. To offer the plea that Luther owed obedience, though true, blunts the issue. It is not a matter of obedience but of truth. In his request for a free and scholarly council Luther was unqualifiedly right. In Rome's rejection of this Rome was unqualifiedly wrong (as many of her most enlightened theologians of the day averred, e.g. Erasmus, Contarini, von Pflug, not to mention contemporary theologians such as Herbert Jedin and Hans Kung). At that fateful hour in January 1521 Leo X finally excommunicated Luther. To the Curia Luther was out of step, yet it could be fairly argued that it was the Curia who was out of step, not Luther.

The reason Luther succeeded where other men and movements had failed lay primarily in Luther's charismatic conversion. The Church needed conversion and neither the jurists nor the humanists could supply the necessary religious impulse even when they diagnosed the malaise rightly. There were plenty of teachers and scholars, but the times needed a religious prophet. That man arose in Martin Luther, one of the people, bone of their bone, flesh of their flesh, a man who spoke their own language, a body of Germany breathing Germany's air. This man had himself lived through their own popular religious life with deep earnestness and truth. He had graduated into the spiritual life as a vocation, and lived it to the full. Yet neither as a young layman, nor yet as a professing monk, could he deliver himself from his burdened conscience. At last he found a gracious God when he discovered that God had found him. By his own personal experience he knew the presence of God, that it was not a matter of God being far away towards whom man must strive by good works, by intellectual effort and by mystic exercises, but of man being alienated from God and God coming all the way to man in his frailty and finitude and alienation. He had discovered the freedom of a Christian man, and, justified by faith, knew a joy no man or circumstance could take away. He became a leader of men, for his joyous faith had released him utterly from all fear of Church, clergy, their threats of hell and blandishments of heaven. He dispelled the vague spiritual fear which had chilled the hearts of men for too long. When they heard Luther talk, when they saw and felt his presence, men knew what faith in God was, and what a joy it was to be a liberated man. Men sensed that it was such a faith they wanted more than anything else.

It has been suggested earlier that twentieth-century man finds it harder to understand Luther's experience of God than all the rest of Luther's intellectual, social and political thinking. Luther had sacrificed a brilliant law career to enter the religious life. In the monastery his fellow monks revered his experience of God, and his superiors were a little abashed at his earnestness and piety. Students, friends, contemporaries and fellow Wittenbergers marvelled at this God-consumed and God-mastered man. His godliness, his perpetual awareness of the living God, humbled many a critic and brought a hushed silence at table. In all that Luther said and did there was this divine dimension, and this was a great secret of his success. This must be granted Luther, be the reader believer or non-believer.

Another secret of Luther's success was his enormous respect

for the common man. No fiery revolutionary, no radical, he moved step by step and explained each step to the common people as he took it. He was one of them, and carried them along with him, so that in the end Luther was doing what they knew wanted doing even if they could never have formulated it. He conserved what they knew to be true to their own experience, and invited them along with him to an experience wider and more far-reaching. These Saxons to whom he belonged, knew him personally as a pious youth, a godly monk, and their brilliant professor. They followed his career breathlessly. He put into words what they had long felt about indulgences but hardly dared say so. And he put it all into good German words which they could understand. He faced Cajetan, confronted Eck, stood his ground before the Emperor. Men now knew that a man who trusts in God need fear neither Pope nor clergy, neither Emperor nor prince. He emancipated from the fear of the Church not only the learned, a relatively simple matter, but all the common people, the one thing needful for a popular reformation and a movement of liberation. So long as the people vaguely believed in the mysterious power which the Church claimed to wield over the temporal and eternal salvation of souls, they were unfree. By sound teaching, and above all by courageous example, Luther convinced the common man that he was safe in God's hands come what may, and not dependent on the blessing of a priestly caste nor lost by its ban. By the time Luther had assured men that they were justified by faith, they were delivered from that medieval dread of Church and priesthood. It was because Luther was free from this dread, and that the people saw he was free yet remained a deeply God-fearing man and churchman, they felt no longer a concern about it, and respected Luther as their great reformer and popular leader. He was a freeman speaking to freedmen.

For these reasons it can be said that Luther was the Reformation, and that its meaning and history can be studied in the record of his spiritual experiences and in the growth of his religious, intellectual and moral convictions. The story of his trial is in one sense the official disavowal and condemnation of Luther's evangelical experience by the Papacy, but before we examine that process we need a brief look at the man himself in the hour of crisis so that we may clothe the issues in his all too ample flesh and blood. Who was this unknown monk who shook the world?

By the year 1517 Luther had become a great power in Wittenberg as a preacher and as a teacher. We are to recall that by then Luther had been a devout monk for some twelve years, obedient, diligent, quiet and pious, greatly approved by his superiors for his learning and his character. He had been entrusted as prior over eleven monasteries in his area, a task he fulfilled with great conscientiousness and considerable courage in the face of recalcitrant or faithless monks. For nearly ten of those years he taught extensively and intensively both Old Testament and New Testament, and had mastered vast areas of historical theology, the fathers, church history and canon law. He was no callow youth, no radical visionary: he was a solid middle-aged man of immense weight and experience and learning.

He was a strong yet simple man, and when called to the town pulpit, he achieved striking success in communicating the Gospel to the 'raw Saxons'. He delivered three or four sermons in the week. Like all great preachers he spoke against the prevalent sins both of the Church and of society. He declaimed against the externalizing of religion into the practice of observances. He preached on the great themes of sin and grace, of the wrath of God as the precursor to God's redeeming love. Above all he expounded the Bible declaring the Word of God to his contemporaries in power and in truth.

If the 'raw Saxons' sitting in the pews sat up and took notice, so did the students in their desks at the University. Luther achieved international fame as a professor and teacher. The lists of matriculation of those years soared, lecture rooms were extended, the university expanded. Even old men from the town matriculated to sit in those desks and to learn more from Friar Martin. Students travelled from every country in Europe.

We are to see this year, 1517, when Luther was thirty-four, as the year that brought Luther out of parochial distinction to world fame. Nevertheless, it is important to see that Luther neither sought nor welcomed this transition. He was a reserved and conscientious monk, of modest birth, simple, pious, intense, occupying a chair of theology, a task he never sought but which was literally imposed on him by his superiors.

He brought to these combined tasks an intellectual wit and a broad Nordic rural humour, devastating in its frankness and flavour. With all this gravity he had a gallant and glad heart, irrepressible, invincible, with a capacity for loyal and warm-hearted friendship. In addition he possessed the intellect of a genius, unique linguistic ability in Latin, German, Greek and Hebrew, and a rare gift of beautiful and powerful language. He was also a first-class musician.

During 1517 Luther had been working on a commentary on Aristotle's *Physics* where he had taken the view that the centrality of Aristotle in the scholastic scheme was actually injurious to biblical theology. (The commentary is no longer extant.) On September 4 he presented some of this thinking in the form of a *Disputation against Scholastic Theology*.

In this document he challenged contemporary scholasticism on the bondage of the will: 'The will is not free to pursue in the light of its own reason any good thing that has been made clear to it' (Thesis 10). He argued that the natural man could not of himself love God but loves only himself and his own interests: 'For the natural man to love God above all else is a figment. It is only a chimera' (Thesis 18). He further argued against the Pelagianism of the schoolmen. Goodness, he urged, comes only from the repentant man who is moved by God's grace. Every man is depraved, and is redeemed only by God's grace: 'The perfectly infallible preparation for grace, the one and only attitude, is the eternal election and predestination of God (Thesis

29). He argued against what he described as the disastrous influence Aristotle had had on Christian ethics and doctrines. In particular he animadverted against Aristotle's point (hardly central to Aristotle) that a man becomes good by doing good. Luther is really after his own emphasis on justification by grace: 'We are not made righteous by doing righteous deeds; but after we have been made righteous we effect righteous deeds' (Thesis 40). 'The whole *Ethics* of Aristotle is the worst enemy of grace' (Thesis 41). He gave a fine series of propositions expounding his evangelical interpretation of Law and Gospel. It is one of the mysteries of historical research that these revolutionary theses seem to have had no repercussions in the academic world, although copies of them were sent to Erfurt and Nurnberg. Yet without doubt this document rather than the Theses against the abuse of indulgences represents Luther's real thrust against Rome. Luther at this hour was just too far ahead of his contemporaries.*

While Luther was lecturing to his students on the *Psalms* and about to begin his monumental lectures on Romans, Leo X was busy raising funds to build St Peter's. The Pope was reluctant to try and draw money from Spain, France or England, but directed three commissions to Germany: the first on 2 December 1514 to an area covering Cologne, Trier and Bremen; the second on 10 January 1515 for Poland and those parts; the third and fateful one for Luther's land, Mainz and Magdeburg, on 31 March 1515.

The circumstances are significant. The young prince Albert of Hohenzollern, though not yet of canonical age (he was twenty-three years old), already held two bishoprics, but coveted the Archbishopric of Mainz, which carried the office of Primate of all Germany. To gain this prize he had to pay for the pallium himself, at the exorbitant price of 20,000 gulden. But the papacy had already milked the diocese of this sum twice in the previous

---

* For a full translation of this document with commentary see James Atkinson, *Library of Christian Classics*, Vol. XVI, pp. 251–73.

ten years and no more could be squeezed out of it. Undeterred, Albert borrowed the money from the Fuggers, the Augsburg bankers, who stipulated as their terms of the bargain that an Indulgence be issued in the diocese spread over a period of eight years, half of the proceeds to go to themselves, half to the Holy See.

Indulgences, even if considered dubious, even meaningless, were not in their early practice scandalous. In the discipline of the tiny minority church of the early centuries the community exercised a strict surveillance of the morals of individual members. Lapses of the faithful had disciplinary punishments imposed by the community. These punishments were often mitigated if the penitent showed a change of heart or his circumstances changed. These mitigations were called indulgences. When in the medieval church this disciplinary practice was corrupted by theories of purgatory, the treasury of merits and the sacrament of penance, and when they could be negotiated for money as Albert was seeking to do, the 'Holy Trade' as it was now technically called, towered as a scandal in Christendom.*

The practice was far worse than the theory. People believed that an indulgence ticket remitted sin, and therefore a man could buy forgiveness and reduce his sentence in purgatory. (The relics in the Castle Church at Wittenberg were reputed to earn a remission of 1,902,202 years and 270 days.) The nefarious traffic was put in the experienced hands of the Dominican monk Tetzel (c. 1465–1519), a remarkable man, half missionary, half charlatan, a stirring rabble rouser of a preacher, with a dash of theological ability. Specimen instructions which he issued to clergy giving details of the practice are extant, as is a specimen indulgence granted for a case of murder by a father of his son, and a specimen sermon.

His rough and ready eloquence gave him a certain popularity.

* For a fuller treatment of indulgences see James Atkinson, *Luther and the Birth of Protestantism*, 1968, pp. 141–48.

Ablaß

In nomine Papae,
auf Lebzeit.

Ich, Kraft der mir anvertrauten apostolischen
Macht, spreche dich los von allen geistlichen Censuren; Ur.
theilssprüchen und Strafen, die du verdient haft, überdies
von allen von dir begangenen Excessen, Sünden und Ver.
brechen, wie groß und schändlich sie auch sein mögen und
um welch Sach willen es auch sei, auch für die unserm
allerheiligsten Vater dem Papste reservirten Fälle.

Ich lösche jeglichen Makel der Untüchtigkeit, alle
Zeichen der Ehelosigkeit aus, die du dabei erhalten ha.
ben magst. Ich erlasse dir die Strafen, die du im Feg.
feuer hättest erdulden müssen. Ich gestatte dir wie.
der die Theilnahme an den kirchlichen Sakramenten.

Ich einverleibe dich wieder der Gemeinschaft der
Heiligen und setze dich in die Unschuld und Reinheit
zurück, in der du zur Stunde deiner Taufe gewesen
bist: So, daß im Augenblick deines Todes das Thor,
durch welches man in den Ort der Qualen und Stra.
fen eingeht, verschlossen bleibt und jenes sich aufthut
welches zum Paradies der Freude führt. Solltest
du nicht bald sterben, so bleibt diese Gnade unerschüt.
terlich bis zu deinem Lebensende.

Im Namen des heiligen Vaters, Amen.

Johann Tietzel,
apostol. Commissarius

In Vollmacht ✠ aller Heiligen
und in Erbarmung gegen Dich, absolvire
Ich Dich von allen Sünden und Missetha.
ten und erlasse Dir alle Strafen auf zehn
Tage.

Johannes Tietzel

1 Two Tetzel indulgences

In the name of the Pope
For the entire life

I, by virtue of the apostolic power entrusted to me, do absolve thee from all ecclesiastical censures, judgements, and punishments which thou must have merited; besides this, from all excesses, sins, and crimes thou mayest have committed, however great and shameful they may have been, and for whatever cause, even in those cases reserved for our most Holy Father the Pope. I obliterate every taint of unvirtues, all signs of infamy, which thou mayest have received. I release thee from all punishments which thou wouldst have endured in purgatory. I permit thee again to participate in the sacraments of the Church. I incorporate thee again in the community of the sanctified, and replace thee in the state of innocence and purity in which thou wert at the hour of thy baptism. So that in the moment of thy death, the door through which the sinner enters the place of torture and punishment will be closed, and that will be open to thee which leads into the paradise of joys. If thou shouldst not soon die, so shall this grace remain unshakable until the end of thy life. In the name of the Holy Father. Amen.

Johann Tietzel, Apostol. Commissarius.

In the authority of all the saints, and in compassion towards thee, I absolve thee from all sins and misdeeds, and remit all punishment for ten days.

Johannes Tietzel

C

In his preaching he deployed heart rending appeals from deceased relations whom he described in vivid terms as writhing in torment in purgatory:

> The dead cry, 'Pity us! Pity us! We are in dire torment from which you can redeem us for a pittance. . . . Will you leave us here in flames? Will you delay our promised glory?'
>> As soon as the coin in the coffer rings
>> The soul from purgatory springs!
>
> Will you not then for a mere sixpenny piece receive these letters of indulgence through which you are able to lead a divine and immortal soul into the fatherland of paradise?

So Tetzel preached and so they believed.

There is a contemporary description of the proceedings given by Myconius: 'He gained by his preaching in Germany an immense sum of money, all of which he sent to Rome; and especially at the new mining works at St Annaberg, where I, Frederick Mecum, heard him for two years, a large sum was collected. It is incredible what this ignorant and impudent friar gave out. He said that if a Christian had slept with his mother, and placed the sum of money in the Pope's indulgence chest, the Pope had power in heaven and earth to forgive the sin, and, if he forgave it, God must do so also. Item, if they contributed readily and brought grace and indulgence, all the hills of St Annaberg would become pure massive silver. Item, so soon as the coin rang in the chest, the soul for whom the money was paid, would go straightway to heaven. The indulgence was so highly prized, that when the commissary entered a city, the Bull was borne on a satin or gold-embroidered cushion, and all the priests and monks, the town council, schoolmaster, scholars, men, women, maidens, and children, went out to meet him with banners and tapers, with songs and procession. Then all the bells were rung, all the organs played; he was conducted into the church, a red cross was erected in the midst of the church, and the Pope's banner displayed; in short, God himself could not have been welcomed and entertained with greater honour.'

Luther stirred. 'I'll knock a hole in his drum,' was his ominous remark when he learned of the proximity of Tetzel's activities. Yet he chose the method least likely to cause any stir. He published 95 theses to promote an academic discussion (exactly as he had done earlier in his concern for scholastic theology), sent a copy to Albert and to his bishop, offering to debate them himself at the university rather than put up a student to do so. Within a month they were all over Germany, and yet in themselves they are simply pithy aphoristic Latin paradoxes promulgated for a few medieval theologians to argue on a matter theologically dubitable and morally offensive.

The contents may be summarized thus: Theses 1–4 showed what the New Testament meant by repentance, viz. the turning of the entire man to God not the 'doing penance' of the Church. Theses 5–7 argued that the Church could remit only her own penalties, God alone could forgive sin. In theses 8–29 he denied the Pope's power over purgatory. In theses 30–40 he explained indulgence and forgiveness. Theses 41–52 argued true works of mercy as against the waste of money in building St Peter's, and theses 53–80 the difference between preaching indulgences and preaching the Gospel. He points out the Pope's responsibility for the scandal in 81–91 and concludes with his own limpid evangelical theology in 92–95.

The galvanic reaction of Europe to these theses startled and disquieted Luther. The subject matter was not one to be aired in a manner over which Luther had no control. Had society wanted a book on indulgences, he growled, he would have written a different document altogether: an academic medieval disputation was wholly inappropriate. Most people praised them and thanked Luther. Dürer sent Luther some woodcuts to mark his appreciation. Yet, many who were sympathetic expressed fear of where it would all lead. The Dominicans openly boasted that they had Luther on the stake: they had simply to settle the time and place.

Luther saw the danger arising from friends as well as foes. He also saw the necessity of educating the populace to the point of judging the issue for themselves. He promptly wrote his *Explanations of the 95 Theses*. All that he had written, he argued, were points of debate, written in accordance with his right and responsibility as a professor of theology: they were not established truths. He claimed that he was arguing an academic disputation: his views were established on Scripture and were not contrary to the authority of the Fathers, canon law and papal decretals. Where they could not be established on these grounds they were in accord with reason and experience. Nevertheless, as a qualified and licenced Doctor of Theology he claimed the right to criticize all scholastic theology, no matter how venerated. He realized he could err, but to err did not make him a heretic. His academic preface to this *Explanations of the 95 Theses**
reads like a clarion call to liberty.

The book went far beyond a mere explanation. It is actually an independent scheme of reform running into 180 pages, a document which terrified his bishop, Scultetus, who did everything to prevent its publication. Every single one of the theses is analysed, explained and justified. Luther actually demanded a reformation, and that it should be the concern not only of the Pope and cardinals, but of the entire Christian world. He discussed the authority of the Pope which he accepted in external matters of order but not in internal matters of faith. He spoke of true historic Catholicism as opposed to the unfounded claims of Rome. He discussed forgiveness as a promise of God and argued against the ecclesiastical and professional possession of it as a priest's to give or withhold, and distinguished sharply between evangelical penitence and ecclesiastical penitence. Indulgences could remit a canonical penalty only, and their use served to screen a soul from the therapeutic power of genuine contrition and to prevent it from

* Full text in *Luther's Works*, Vol. 31, pp. 79–252.

finding any real penitence. The treasury of merits he ruled out; the Church had but one treasure, and that was Christ.

Luther's concern was to make Christendom aware of her wholesale defection from New Testament Christianity and of her appalling theological ignorance. He thought that if men's hearts and minds were opened to an awareness of this, God would instigate a reformation in and through that awareness. Luther's explanations show scholarship and ability, as well as a grasp of canon law, church history and the writings of the Church Fathers.

The book is much too long to be quoted at any length, though it comprises an integral part in the Luther case. The quotation which follows, which is an explanation of the first thesis, gives a fair example of Luther's method, embracing as it does, exact linguistic analysis of the words involved, a broad spectrum of biblical evidence, supported by rational argument and the evidence of experience. The book is written in Latin and was directed to clergy and scholars, not to the people.

> When our Lord and Master Jesus Christ said, 'Repent' (Matt. 4.17), he willed the entire life of believers to be one of repentance. This I assert and in no way doubt.
>
> 1. Nevertheless, I shall prove the thesis for the sake of those who are uninformed, first from the Greek word *metanoeite* itself, which means 'repent' and could be translated more exactly by the Latin *transmentamini*, which means 'assume another mind and feeling, recover one's senses, make a transition from one state of mind to another, have a change of spirit'; so that those who hitherto have been aware of earthly matters may now know the spiritual, as the Apostle says in Rom. 12.2, 'Be transformed by the renewal of your mind.' By this recovery of one's senses it happens that the sinner has a change of heart and hates his sin.
>
> It is evident, however, that this recovery or hatred of oneself should involve one's whole life, according to the passage,

'He who hates his soul in this life, preserves it for eternal life' (Matt. 10.39). And again, 'He who does not take his cross and follow me, is not worthy of me' (Matt. 10.38). And in the same chapter, 'I have not come to bring peace, but a sword' (Matt. 10.34). In Matt. 5.4, 'Blessed are those who mourn, for they shall be comforted.' And Paul in Romans 6 and 8 and in many other places orders us to mortify the flesh and members of the body which are upon earth. In Gal. 5.24 he teaches us to crucify the flesh with its lustful desires. In II Corinthians 6 he says, 'Let us show ourselves in much patience, in many fastings, etc.' (Cf. II Cor. 6.45). I produce these citations so extensively because I am dealing with those who are unacquainted with our teachings.

2. I shall prove this thesis also according to reason. Since Christ is the master of the spirit, not of the letter, and since his words are life and spirit (John 6.63), He must teach the kind of repentance which is done in spirit and in truth, but not that which the most arrogant hypocrites could do openly by distorting their faces in fasts and by praying in streets and heralding their giving of alms (Matt. 6.16). Christ must teach a repentance, I say, which can be done in every walk of life, a repentance which the king in purple robes, the priest in his elegance, and the princes in their dignity can do just as well as the monk in his rituals and the mendicant in his poverty, just as Daniel and his companions did in Babylon (Dan. 1 and 3). For the teaching of Christ must apply to all men, that is, to men in every walk of life.

3. We pray throughout our whole life and we must pray 'forgive us our debts' (Matt. 6.12); therefore, we repent throughout our whole life and are displeased with ourselves, unless anyone may be so foolish as to think that he must pretend to pray for the forgiveness of debts. For the debts for which we are commanded to pray are real and not to be treated lightly; and even if they were venial, we could not be saved unless they were remitted.

The ecclesiastics and the Dominicans (the champions of orthodoxy and papal absolutism) made the fatal and fateful step of
standing for the Pope and the authority of the Church against
individual criticism and conviction, even against plain learning.
Luther's opponents taught him more than his friends. The
Dominicans in Saxony met at Frankfurt-on-Oder in January 1518
where Tetzel debated his theses written as counter-theses to
Luther's 95. Luther was not answered but condemned, and all
the old assertions repeated with still more verve. Whereas Tetzel
had earlier asserted 'As soon as the coin in the coffer rings, the
soul from purgatory springs' he now declared that the indulgence
was so efficacious that the release of the tortured soul actually
took place '*before*' the coin in the coffer rings. In fact grave
assurances were given that an indulgence would absolve even
the enormity of the violation of the Blessed Virgin Mary. With
friends of Tetzel's calibre the papal curia had no need of enemies.
Whereas Luther first thought that the Pope would thank him for
his great service to the Church, it became clear to him that
the papal henchmen had only one purpose, to preserve the papacy
right or wrong, and their place in it, and at the same time to
calumniate every opponent unheard and unrefuted.

Luther counter-attacked with a popular tract, which brought
the debate before the layman:

> Let none of you procure tickets of indulgence. Leave that to
> the lazy Christians dozing half asleep. You go right ahead
> without them. . . . I know nothing about souls dragged out of
> purgatory by an indulgence. I do not even believe it, in spite
> of all the new-fangled doctors who say so. But you cannot
> prove it to them. The Church has not even made up its
> mind in the matter yet.

And concludes,

> On these points [against indulgences] I have no doubt at all.
> They [indulgences] are not properly based on scripture. There-
> fore, have no doubt about them, regardless of what the

scholastic doctors say. . . . I pay no attention to that sort of
drivel, for nobody engages on it except a few dunderheads
who have never even smelt a Bible nor read any Christian
teachers.

Tetzel was no match for Luther who disabused him of his wild
and ignorant calumnies of heresy and apostasy. He dismissed his
scholarship and accused him of handling the Scriptures like a
sow a bag of oats.

Reference was made above to Luther's enemies being his best
teachers. They compelled him to think again on the Church
and the papacy in the light of scripture, history and his own
experience. Tetzel and his supporters held papal power so
blatantly and in such absolute, unqualified terms that Luther
re-examined the entire matter in terms of biblical scholarship
and historical criticism.

It was argued that the Pope was supreme over Church and
Council, inerrant and above the Scripture. He was infallible,
and himself alone, not the Church, possessed the keys of Peter.
The Church possessed all truth, and whatsoever it teaches, with
or without Patristic or Scriptural authority, is to be believed, not
only theology but practice. For anybody to doubt this, or detract
from this, even to interpret the Scriptures differently, is to
be guilty of heresy. Anyone undermining the authority of the
Church, or its spokesmen, is equally a heretic.

A former friend, the distinguished theologian and disputant,
John Eck (about whom we shall learn more in the developments
of the next year), without warning undertook a venomous and
virulent attack against Luther, repeating essentially the views
expressed in the previous paragraph. Luther argued that these
blind schoolmen were opposing him because he preferred the
Bible and the Fathers to scholasticism, and because he had the
audacity to follow St Paul's advice, 'Prove all things' (I Thess
5.21). Eck later explained that what he had written were private
notes and not a document for publication, true enough, and

Luther amicably closed the issue by not publishing his own reply and sending Eck a copy of the manuscript.

Rome was now alerted. Following the report on the affair by the Archbishop of Mainz, the Pope consulted Cardinal Cajetan, General of the Dominican Order, a scholarly and good man who was to play an important role in Luther's trial. Though a strict curialist he responded to the Pope with a reasoned statement on the various views on indulgences held by theologians and considered there was no ground for the charge of heresy in Luther's theses. But the Dominicans found a more amenable access to the Pope through a cousin, Giulio di Medici. The Pope was persuaded by him to ask Gabriel della Volta, already nominated as the next General of the Augustinians, to restrain Luther from further agitation. This della Volta did by writing to Staupitz, Luther's Vicar General, to call his subordinate to theological account. Meanwhile Luther's diocesan bishop very courteously asked Luther to defer from further controversy. It was Volta's plan that at the next chapter of the Augustinians to be held in Heidelberg in April 1518 that the Order would exact Luther's submission, failing which, send him to Rome for trial.*

At great personal danger Luther walked all the way to Heidelberg to face the consequences. Here he was not to play the part of the accused heretic, but the role of theologian and apologist.

The debate was an unqualified triumph for Luther. Luther dealt with the great theological themes he had been making his own: God's righteousness and man's righteousness; Law and Gospel; sin, grace, free will and faith; justification by works and justification in Christ; man's inability to will and do the good on his own strength; in particular, his powerful theology of the cross. Here are all the essentials of Luther's mighty evangelical theology, and in many cases they are carefully developed. And when he had concluded he dealt with the

* For a full translation with comment of the Heidelberg Disputation see James Atkinson, *Library of Christian Classics*, Vol. XVI, pp. 276–307.

erroneous Aristotelian scholastic philosophy. Luther stood as a theologian before theologians, religious man before religious men. He was treated with courtesy and respect, and given a considerate hearing.

On his return to Wittenberg the good Staupitz was anxious to catch the changing tide at the full, and persuaded Luther to write to the Pope explaining his position. In his letter he is very humble, but carries the theological war into the enemies' camp. He repudiates the charges of heresy and sedition and argues his theological responsibility to deal with these issues. He indicates the support he has from his own university and from his prince, and argues that Christendom is offended and revolted at its leadership and is demanding a day of reckoning. He included a fuller exposition of his theses. Here he went into detail on the corruption and morals of Rome, criticized papal power and absolutism, developed his protest against indulgences, called for a General Council and a reformation of the Church not simply by councils but by the whole of Christendom, under the power of God. The movement which had begun as a simple unassailable criticism of an intolerable abuse which continued to shock every decent mind in Europe, lay and clerical alike, had now developed into a total criticism of contemporary theology and practice. Luther had not only challenged the scandalous abuse of indulgences but was now effectively demolishing Thomas, Aristotle and the schoolmen and replacing them with a Biblical and Patristic theology based on historical and linguistic analyses.

Papal prosecution of Luther; Citation to Rome

Foiled in their attempts to effect Luther's submission in Germany, the Dominicans pressed the Curia to take cognizance of Luther's activities. Pope Leo commissioned Prierias, the Master of the Sacred Palace and an Inquisitor, to cite Luther, in accordance with canon law, to appear at Rome in person, and to be examined on suspicion of heresy and as perverter of the papal power.

Prierias was a Dominican and a reactionary obscurantist, now utterly suspect by both the learned world and the humanists for his handling of the Reuchlin affair. True to form he enclosed with his official citation a document in criticism of Luther's position in which he haughtily claimed that he had taken a mere matter of three days to dismiss Luther. His starting point was the absolute and infallible power of the Pope who had the authority to compel the secular arm to take action against anybody holding other views. The Pope had no reason either to account for his decisions to anybody or to discuss the heretic's views. The whole is a dogmatic reassertion of papalism interspersed with threats to Luther and gross abuse. The citation enclosed ordered Luther to appear at Rome within sixty days of its receipt to answer charges as a heretic and rebel against ecclesiastical power.

Document and citation were despatched to Cardinal Cajetan, papal legate at the Diet of Augsburg. Cajetan forwarded them to Wittenberg where they arrived on 7th August. But Luther was not prepared to have his case argued in such a vulgar, prejudiced, obscurantist climate. Luther and everybody else realized that were he to go to Rome he would never return but must expect the fate of John Huss. He also penned a reply to Prierias, courteous but trenchant. Luther knew that he was engaged in answering not a mere academic disputation but an official challenge from Rome, and had opened the missive with its official seal with trembling hands. Luther's anxiety and fear turned to ridicule when he read the dialogue of Prierias. Luther came out openly against the papist theology. He boldly refutes the Thomist and papalist doctrine of the Church as embodied in the Roman Church and the papacy. He argues for a doctrine based on Scripture, and Fathers and sound reason. He challenges the infallible authority of the Pope on faith and morals, and instances Julius II and his bloody bellicosity, and Boniface VIII who 'entered the Church as a wolf, governed it as a lion, and died like a dog'. Pope and Council may err, though both may have appropriate respect. The Church to Luther exists only in Christ, and its appropriate representative, a proper Council.

Luther knew that for all the support of his university colleagues, and of countless other academics, Rome with all its power structures behind it, had acted against him. The situation was now quite different. He realized his only hope was lay protection. He sought this of his own Elector, Frederick the Wise, writing also to his court chaplain Spalatin (a former fellow student at Erfurt) and hoping Maximilian I would counter his extradition to Rome.

At this moment his Dominican opponents played a very mean trick. Luther had further developed his criticisms in his sermon on 'Excommunication'. Invited out to supper at the house of Dr Emser at Dresden he had warmly defended his position and expressed his views on the papal ban as a weapon of fear now far removed from its original nature of a spiritual discipline. Unknown to him a Dominican monk was hiding behind a curtain taking down all the racy comments of which Luther allowed himself the indulgence in a private party. These notes were taken post-haste to Augsburg, doctored up into theses, and circulated at the Diet in Luther's name. This forgery did irrevokable harm to Luther's cause, as its perpetrators intended.

On reading the documents purporting to be a statement of Luther to the Diet, Maximilian turned against Luther, slyly hinting that Frederick lay behind this. The aged Maximilian was now playing all his cards to persuade the Pope to support the candidature of his grandson, Charles of Spain, to succeed him as Emperor, but Philip was the one man the Pope did not want. Maximilian begged the Pope to intervene at once against such damnable and heretical views to the honour of God and the salvation of the faithful. Luther's one hope was the Elector (supported perhaps by the Emperor) but his enemies had destroyed this last defence in that they had secured the support of a greater than the Elector. Nevertheless, it should never be lost sight of that the Diet was more than the Emperor. The evidence for the real feeling of the Diet as one of intolerable resentment against the papal exactions is overwhelming (RA II 661–718) and this immense lay dissatisfaction played an important part in Luther's trial.

But the Elector was no fool. He was also a fair-minded man, determined that justice would be meted out to Luther and felt in honour bound to protect his professor from injustice. His lawyers came to Luther's help to protect him from Dominican machinations. They advised Luther to request a safe conduct from the Elector to allow him to go to Rome, knowing that the Elector would decline and thereby afford Luther a weighty excuse to defer the citation to Rome.

Luther before Cajetan

The Emperor's letter to the Pope produced a deep impression and created a new situation in that Luther's heresy had now grown into notoriety. Knowing the Emperor supported him against Luther the Pope discarded the earlier citation to Rome on the grounds that Luther had made the situation much worse by his continued writing and speaking. The Pope commanded Cajetan in a letter dated 23rd August to summon Luther before him forthwith, and by the aid of the secular arm, to compel him to appear and to hold him in captivity pending further instructions. If Luther comes of his own will and recants, Cajetan is empowered to receive him into mother Church. If he refuses, Luther and his adherents are to be cut off from the Church by public edict. All authorities are bound to apprehend Luther: any authority giving Luther any kind of aid or protection will incur an interdict.

On the same day the Pope wrote to the Elector implying that 'that son of iniquity' was behaving the way he was only because he presumed on the protection of his lay lord. Frederick was requested to see that Luther was delivered to Rome for judgment. More indicative of the Pope's mind was the letter sent, also on the same date, to the provincial head of the Augustinians in Germany. This letter ordered the Vicar General (Gerhard Hicker) to arrest and detain Luther, chained hand and foot, in custody under penalty of excommunication and interdict for all who disobeyed.

This new hostile tone arose from the fact that Luther was now a notorious heretic and canon law allowed peremptory and unconditional submission for such a category: there need be neither enquiry nor trial. Already the tragedy of the Roman process had set in. No attempt to hear Luther, just the necessity to silence him. Strong as the papacy was in Christendom as a whole, in Germany fatal cracks were now yawning wide. The grasping secularism of the papacy, its corruption, its oppression had weakened its hold on the German mind. Had the papacy heeded Luther's responsible, informed, spiritual and academic criticism, the papacy might have prevented the division of Christendom. Further, Rome ought to have realized the tight limitation of the powers of the Emperor: he was but the chairman of a group of princes, without whose co-operation he had no executive power. Any continuous reading of the minutes of the Diet will show how effective the power of the princes was, and how powerless the Emperor was without their goodwill and cooperation. In this case, Luther's prince was far and away the cleverest and most powerful of them all, and was not likely to be outmanoeuvred. He also carried considerable authority by virtue of his fair-mindedness and integrity.

Frederick responded to the Pope's high-handed and arbitrary handling of the crisis by approaching Cajetan to counter this move and to get back to the *status quo ante* when Luther had requested a full, fair and free hearing. Luther had since made plain in writing that he had no desire at all to compromise his prince by soliciting his support, but only that his prince protect him from the violence of summary arrest and condemnation.

Frederick found Cajetan a far more responsible man than the Pope and the rest of the Dominican yap dogs. The Cardinal was a scholar in his own right, untainted by the scandalous secularism and corruption of his fellows, and not uncritical of the Dominican rabble. He did not grant all that the Elector sought, namely a fair trial and examination before a competent and impartial German tribunal, but promised him a 'fatherly hearing' before himself at Augsburg.

A political issue was also influencing the Pope in allowing Cajetan's conciliatory plan of action. Maximilian was concerned that his grandson, Charles of Spain, should succeed him. He had contrived the support of five of the Electors, only Frederick and the Elector of Trier stood apart. The Pope did not want the young Charles, who was already King of Naples, to be Emperor, since this would conflict with the Pope's secular interests in Italy. The Pope, therefore, sought to conciliate Frederick by adopting a kindlier tone towards Luther. Accordingly on 11 September the Pope wrote to Cajetan empowering him, through the Elector, to examine Luther, pronounce his verdict on the case, without allowing himself to be drawn into a disputation. If Luther were prepared to abjure his errors, Cajetan was empowered to rehabilitate Luther. The papal brief of 23 August (p. 45) was still in force, but was in temporary abeyance to allow the Cardinal to hear Luther and meet his Elector's request.

With a complete set of credentials and a safe conduct through Frederick's dominions, strengthened by supporting papers from his university, Luther set off on foot with Leonard Beier for Augsburg on 26 September. His Elector sent him twenty gold florins for the journey. Luther's heart was full of foreboding. Spalatin had led him to expect a full hearing before a German tribunal, but what he had received was a summons to appear before an Italian cardinal, and a Dominican to boot. This was one of Luther's darkest hours. In his final trial he was to stand strong in the sense of half Germany being on his side as well as most of the academic world, but now he was defenceless, facing a situation of which he had been given no information. He was torn with uncertainties on the long journey and arrived in a serious state of nervous and physical exhaustion. He had to be carried the last few miles. The prior at Weimar warned him that he was walking into a trap: he would face the stake at Augsburg. Others offered the same opinion and begged him to return to the safety of his own country. As he entered Augsburg he was later to say that the Devil tormented him with doubts. 'But yet I stood fast,' he wrote, as he was to do later at Worms. If it was God's cause, he argued it was bound to win: if God did not take it up, nothing Luther could do would make it succeed.

To his astonishment, and to Cajetan's disdain, neither Link nor Frederick's counsellors would let Luther out of their sight until they had secured the imperial safe conduct. This procured (11 October), they warned Luther not to be deceived by the Cardinal's courtesy, for his real attitude to Luther was one of bitter hostility. Luther was much enheartened now to learn of the strong support for him from the senate and citizens of Augsburg.

Cajetan sent an Italian diplomat to Luther, Serralonga by name, to indicate that he would meet the simple request for recantation and be given no opportunity to discuss the case with the Cardinal. Serralonga sought to reassure Luther on how well disposed the Cardinal was to him, and strongly urged Luther on several visits to yield. 'Six letters will save you,' he flamboyantly urged Luther—*revoco,* I recant. Luther replied he would be the first to say them, if he was convinced of his error. The idea of the monk arguing with the Cardinal was inconceivable to Serralonga. He warned Luther not to expect support from Frederick to the extent of taking up arms for Luther's cause. Luther was horrified at the thought. 'Where will you be in that event, then?' Serralonga demanded. 'Where I am now,' Luther replied, 'in heaven.' He wrote a splendid letter to

Luther as an Augustinian Friar, 1520
from an engraving by Lucas Cranach the Elder

3 Cardinal Albrecht of Brandenburg, 1520
From an engraving by Lucas Cranach the Elder

4 John Tetzel
From an engraving by Brühl

Melanchthon in Wittenberg assuring him that for his sake and the students he had left behind, he would stand his ground.

On 12 October Luther was ushered in before the Cardinal, whom he found gracious and courteous.* At once Luther apologized for any temerity of which he was guilty and expressed his willingness to reconsider his opinions. This attitude Cajetan warmly commended and genuinely set out to settle the matter in a pastoral manner. Cajetan was a very different kind of Dominican from those who had so far opposed Luther with their wild, emotional, non-intellectual attitude, yet Cajetan was equally a prisoner of ecclesiasticism, in that, in spite of his scholarship and spirituality, he was not free to handle the matter in a fatherly way and discuss as with a son the nature and content of Luther's protest.

Cajetan's first move, in fact the only move his principles allowed him, was to present Luther with an ultimatum. In accordance with his mandate from the Pope, he required unconditional revocation, without discussion, and assurances that Luther would never raise these issues again in the Church nor ever again disturb the peace of the Church. Luther asked to see the mandate. The Cardinal was unable to grant the request. Luther testily averred that he had not walked all the way from Wittenberg to be told to recant and keep silent. He asked what his errors were.

Still maintaining his dignity and his 'fatherly' tone, Cajetan gave two instances. The first, Luther's views on the Treasury of Merits (Thesis 58), the second, his views on the sacrament of penance (Thesis 7) where Luther argued it was not the sacrament which justified but faith. The former was plainly incompatible with the Papal Bull *Unigenitus* of Clement VI (1343) which affirmed that Christ had acquired for the Church an infinite treasure, to which the Virgin and the saints had added their contributions, a treasure committed by Christ to Peter and

* For a full account of the hearing before Cajetan see *Luther's Works*, Vol. 31, pp. 255–92.

D

his successors for the benefit of the faithful. As for the latter
view it was plainly novel and erroneous to assert the necessity
of faith to the efficacy of absolution in Penance. Cajetan argued
that the view was contrary to scripture in that it made grace
dependent on faith. On these two grounds alone Luther
must revoke his views both on indulgences as well as on justification by faith.

The Cardinal had haughtily underestimated his man, 'this
shabby, little friar' as he dubbed him. If Cajetan were prepared
to settle questions of truth by reference to papal bull and
ecclesiastical belief, Luther was not. Luther had wrestled with
God and religious experience for years, and out of it all had
developed a considerable authority based not on scholastic
authorities but on truth tested by Scripture, experience and
reason. On the first issue of the Treasury of Merits Luther
argued that it was a sheer distortion of Scripture. Cajetan warmly
rejoined by insisting on the inerrant and absolute power of the
Pope, who was above both Scripture and Council. This Luther
stoutly denied, quoting the University of Paris in support.

It was the second point which brought the argument from
the fencing of sophistries to the heart beat of Luther's protest,
namely, justification by faith. The cardinal maintained the
Thomist view of the efficacy of sacramental grace, arguing that
this was also scriptural. Luther countered with his clear biblical
view of justification by faith in Christ alone, marshalling an
immense weight of scriptural evidence and challenging Cajetan
to disprove his case from the same source. To give way on
this issue was to Luther tantamount to a denial of Christ. Neither
yielded.

On the following day (13 October) Luther appeared with a
written statement, composed on the advice of his counsellors.
He was attended by Staupitz, a notary and four imperial
councillors. In the document Luther reasserted that none of
his teaching was against the Catholic Church, but, if it were, he
was ready to renounce it. He argued that his concern had been

truth, and a pursuit of this kind could not be given up unless he were heard, and convinced by those who said he was wrong. He averred that he was unaware of anything he had taught which was contrary to Scripture, the Fathers, the decretals and sound reason, but on the contrary believed his theology to be sound, true and Catholic. He knew that he could err and was fully open to debate and disputation. If the Cardinal felt unable to grant him this opportunity to free criticism in open debate, he would answer the Cardinal's criticisms in writing and refer this statement to the judgment and opinion of the Universities of Basle, Freiburg, Louvain or Paris. In fact, all that Luther had wanted all along was the arbitration of an impartial and competent tribunal. This suggestion was a harsh cut, for it implied that Cajetan was either incompetent or not free to make any judgment, except to enunciate the Curial prejudgment.

This request exceeded the bounds of the Cardinal's commission. In the same kindly manner of yesterday he repeated the request for an unconditional recantation, advising Luther to desist from his insane plan. Luther then asked for permission to hand in a written statement for the battle of words of the previous day had got them nowhere. The term 'battle' incensed Cajetan—he had not come to dispute and to do battle, he said, but to hear Luther kindly, to admonish him, and even to make reconciliation with the Pope and the Church. Staupitz intervened, in an attempt to save the situation, with a request to the Cardinal to accede to Luther's being allowed to submit a written statement. The Cardinal, still hoping for a successful outcome, agreed reluctantly but kindly.

On the next day (14 October), in company with Feilitzsch and Ruhel as representatives of the Elector, Luther presented a detailed exposition of the two points on the efficacy of the sacrament and on justification by faith. Luther re-stated his views that Popes might err and had erred, that their decrees were acceptable only in so far as they were in accordance with Scripture, that the Fathers were right to assert that a council was superior to a Pope and that the present Pope and his Fifth Lateran Council were wrong to abrogate Basle. The opinion even of any individual Christian, if based on Scripture and reason, may be preferred to a papal decretal. He argued that justification by faith was scriptural, and without faith the sacrament of penance brought a Christian to damnation. Above all, no man could ever be asked to violate his conscience.

Luther's statement incensed Cajetan. He treated it contemptuously, raised his voice, repeated his views on the points in dispute, demanded Luther's recantation and threatened him with the full scale of the Church's penalties. Luther could not get a word in, so he shouted too. The Cardinal shouted harder, ordered Luther out, and told him never to come into his presence again, except with a recantation in his hand.

So ended Luther's first appearance and examination before the authority of the Church. Luther was now in an acutely dangerous position, and all his advisers were bewildered and nonplussed. Nevertheless, the Cardinal made one further effort. He sent for Staupitz, begged him to persuade Luther to recant, offering a form of recantation. But Staupitz assured Cajetan that Luther would not change except on scriptural proof. Staupitz, supported by Link, begged Luther to write a humble, respectful letter, confessing that in the heat of the moment he had spoken of the Pope indiscreetly and irreverently, to beg forgiveness, and to promise silence if his enemies would remain quiet. Further, to say that he would recant at the command of his Vicar-General, though not on a basis of Thomistic opinions which were not an adequate basis for any theology. He begged the Cardinal to refer the whole case to the Pope to give everybody time to go further into the doubtful points and when the Church thus spoke, Luther would hear and obey. All this amounted to was a simple and courteous summary of what he had said more strongly in argument, an eirenic statement which bore the touches of the good and gentle Staupitz and of Link.

This promising development was received with blank silence.

Two whole days Staupitz remained in nervous expectation. The older man sensed that all hope had gone. He combed Augsburg unsuccessfully to raise secretly enough funds to get Luther out of the country into the safer academic milieu of the University of Paris, already strongly anti-papal. He wrote to his Elector, saying that Cajetan was threatening to break Luther and to throw them both into prison. Staupitz had all along striven to play the role of mediator of Luther to the Church, and now was compelled to realize that he had failed and saw no way out of the situation. He released Luther from his vows and in company with Link beat a hasty and fearful retreat out of Augsburg, without even taking his leave of the Cardinal, but saying to Luther, 'Remember, you began this affair in the name of our Lord Jesus Christ.'

Luther now stood dangerously alone. He made a last minute bid on 18 October by writing 'to the Pope ill-informed who ought to be better informed', as he expressed it. He demanded a hearing elsewhere than in Rome, making the point that as the Pope himself had only narrowly escaped assassination in Rome the previous year, the chances were that he, Luther, would not. He wrote again to Cajetan taking formal leave. No answer was returned. Luther's supporters interpreted the contrivance of this ominous silence with dark forebodings. Very ugly rumours on Luther's fate began to circulate, and to gain credence.

In this atmosphere Luther was awakened at dead of night on 20–21 October, by a trusty attendant sent by his friend Langenmantel, a canon of the cathedral. He was whisked out of a postern gate, thrown on to a horse which he had to ride without breeches and without boots. Without a stop he was galloped through the dark night to a village called Murheim, forty miles away. When he reached the stable he fell off his horse in an agony of pain and weakness and had to remain there in the stable with his horse a whole day before he recovered strength to move. He set off for Wittenberg through Nürnberg, where he was warmly received. There he received a copy of his arrest, a document which brought home to him the narrowness of his escape.

Sequel to the Augsburg hearing

On his return to Wittenberg Luther wrote an account of his hearing and decided to appeal direct to a General Council before which he might freely plead his cause. Not intending it for immediate publication he ordered the document to be held in readiness against the Pope's anticipated action. It was published without Luther's knowledge and to Frederick's embarrassment.

Luther had now no legal ground on which to stand. He had been declared a notorious heretic, and by canon law such a person has no right of appeal. Further, by the Bull *Execrabilis* 1460 it was a heretical act to appeal direct to a General Council. This action of Luther made Frederick's efforts to protect him extraordinarily delicate.

Meanwhile, Cajetan, moved by Luther's protests, wrote to the Pope a further study of indulgences with a report on the Luther affair (25 October). The Curia converted this into a decretal (9 November) which was entrusted to Miltitz to be conveyed to the Cardinal. The decretal was pointedly directed against 'a certain religious in Germany' and was a restatement of the power of the keys and the validity of indulgences with the express command to make it known throughout Germany. This document made it plain that Luther's interpretation of the Bull *Unigenitus* was erroneous and that his contentions on the subject were inadmissible. If Luther persisted in maintaining either, he was thereby excommunicated. The Bull simply assumes the validity of the Thomist-Dominican interpretation of the theory of indulgences and the absolute power and infallibility of the Pope in this matter. No attempt is made to meet or even to consider the objections Luther made: no reference to the sordid scandals associated with the revolting money-making affair. Cajetan had simply rehashed the questionable though conventional Thomist doctrine and covered over all the objections and scandals in deference to the Curia and the fanatical

Dominicans who were now licking their wounds. This statement was no answer to Luther neither did it satisfy Frederick.

Rumours began to proliferate as they do in anxious and uncertain situations. It was openly said that Rome had now made up her mind to extirpate the Lutheran heresy and its author. Luther was willing to go into banishment, and every sermon he preached was thought to be his last. Some of his friends suggested that the Elector himself should take him into the safe custody of his castle. The Elector was put into the invidious position of either abandoning Luther or defying the Pope. He wanted neither, but Cajetan's blunt letter from Augsburg and Miltitz dangling his promises and bribes before him did not help. Luther was always prepared to fight it out—on other grounds— to save his own Elector from hurt and embarrassment. It was at this stage that Luther published his *Acta Augustana* (an account of his hearing at Augsburg), and the printer issued his *Appeal to a Council*. Frederick was walking a tight-rope. Whatever the worth of all the rumours and the weight of the various suggestions, one thing emerges with certainty, and that is Frederick's rugged determination to protect Luther from his enemies at all cost.

On 8 December Frederick replied to Cajetan. He enclosed Luther's criticism of Cajetan's statements, and refused either to banish Luther or to hand him over to Rome. He pointed out that the entire university was behind Luther and had begged him to protect Luther from his enemies and to seek for him a fair trial. He himself as a Christian prince would act in honour and good conscience. How could he adjudge a man a heretic when not convicted of heresy?

It is worth surveying the proceedings against Luther thus far. Such a survey opens up the issues of the case as it was finally to disclose itself in Worms 1521, and takes on the nature of a preliminary trial before a lower court.

It is of special interest and particular significance that in the two occasions when Luther was summoned to appear, the one before Cardinal Cajetan at the Diet of Augsburg 1518 the other before the Emperor at the Diet of Worms 1521, that the plan of Rome in both cases was to summon him to recant only and to allow him no opportunity to speak, argue or debate. To modern ears procedure of such a kind makes a mockery of justice and gives the very phrase 'The Hearing of Luther' a meaning bordering on ridicule. Countless Germans of the sixteenth century felt the same, not the least their champion Luther, a fearless intellectual, the most dangerous of combinations in a leader. What is still more surprising, when Rome determined at stage two to put up its most redoubtable disputant in the field to crush the Wittenberg Theology in open debate at the University of Leipzig in 1519 (p. 60), Luther himself was not even invited to the debate! Instead, Eck challenged a colleague of Luther to debate, Carlstadt, an older dull-witted man, slow in speech, with no confidence in dispute, and what was worse, a man who mixed up the new evangelical theology with a mass of vague popular socialist anarchistic radicalism. Carlstadt was a 'hippy' of the early sixteenth century: he later actually threw off his academic gown, donned a peasant's smock, married a very young girl, and went back to the land. Carlstadt would be trounced by Eck, and trounced publicly and cheaply: it would be a public thrashing. And so it turned out.

On these three occasions, Augsburg 1518, Leipzig 1519, Worms 1521, Rome was determined that Luther should not speak. At Augsburg he provoked the Cardinal to argument and managed to state his case in spoken and in written word. At Leipzig he contrived to get on the cart uninvited and actually appeared at the end of the debate. At Worms, by a brilliant and courteous request for twenty four hours' reflection, a request granted with considerable misgiving and concern, Luther freed himself from his counsellors, and untrammelled, gave his famous defence, and uttered before the world and all history, and all posterity those stirring last words, 'Here I stand!'.

It is disturbing to modern ears that the Roman authorities sought only to silence Luther, never to hear him, but it must be recalled that Luther was under a vow of obedience. Further, it is essential to set the debate in the sixteenth century not the twentieth. Rome believed that her authority was infallible. Luther questioned this authority. Therefore Luther was wrong, and if he would not be silent he had to be silenced. This simple syllogism sums up the whole of the papalist decision. Nevertheless, as a doctor of theology under oath, Luther had the right and duty to speak, even against his monastic vows and his duty of obedience to the hierarchy and the Church (WA 30.3.522. 2–8. 1532).

In the document which Luther left behind him at Augsburg, he merely restated the position already expressed in debate and in writing. To sum up: he restated that his attack on the scandalous traffic in indulgences was justified and permissible to a theologian, and that his protest constituted true Catholic practice; the charge of heresy was without substance, he was a true Catholic; that sound reasons were adduced to justify his refusal to present himself at Rome; he objected to the manner of the Cardinal's handling of the case for he was given no 'hearing' at all; he indicated that he was to make an appeal to the Pope, showing his willingness to be obedient to proper and lawful authority.

All this is true enough, but there is a great deal to be said for Cajetan. Cajetan's commission did not allow him to handle the Luther affair as an open question, subject to debate. More than that, Cajetan's own theological position as a Thomist and a papalist forbade him *ab initio* from any kind of admission that there may be something in what Luther was saying. To him the Pope and the Church were infallible: if Luther disagreed Luther was dead wrong. Therefore, Luther had to be silent or be silenced. There was nothing in the Lutheran theology that could be appropriately discussed. On these two grounds Cajetan remained immovable. Further, Cajetan went to the trouble of

reading Luther's writings, and certainly made the attempt to
handle Luther, as he promised, in a 'fatherly' way, not as a
judge. Cajetan was a good and godly cleric, unlike most of his
contemporaries, secularized, greedy, grasping. He was never
guilty of the rabid emotionalism which characterized the
Dominican move against Luther. If Cajetan was wrong in the
debate, he nevertheless argued his case cogently and kindly
where he need only have issued instructions. He reacted sharply
when Luther suddenly left Augsburg, hurt to the quick. It was
fear that had pressed Luther's friends to spirit him out of
Augsburg where no good could come to him, though there is no
evidence in Cajetan's life and conduct which could have caused
the Luther supporters to fear violence. Luther did not. Cajetan
was an honourable man and certainly respected Frederick's
concern that Luther have a fair hearing.

In fact, Cajetan represented the old setting sun of papal
infallibility, an authority to be imposed on men in rigid
obedience at whatever cost of intellectual and spiritual integrity.
Luther represented the new rising sun of the authority of truth
openly questioned and freely arrived at by the collective people
of God in free debate and clear conscience. Cajetan insisted that
all truth belonged to Catholic tradition and stressed papal
authority, docility and obedience. Luther sought to move
authority from this static conception to a dynamic and developing one untrammelled by traditional theological opinion, to
follow Scripture, study tradition and obey one's conscience in
the light of free learning. In Cajetan and Luther the old met
the young: the old refused to listen and the young left home.

Further, Cajetan was indubitably right when he stated his
own position to the Elector, that whereas Luther had argued
that he was simply defending the views expressed in his theses,
the Luther he faced was a different Luther, a Luther who had
in subsequent writings argued his views as indisputably true and
who had made considerable theological advance. Luther had
spoken against both the Apostolic See as well as the Catholic

Church. He had no choice as the Pope's representative but to condemn Luther and, further, to ask the Elector to hand over such a person to Rome, or else banish him from the country.

What Luther was in fact asking of Rome was to surrender the papacy in the absolute and totalitarian role it had assumed, a sacrifice it should make in the name of Scripture, conscience and reason. The papacy sensed this was a gathering up of all the ancient reformers from William of Occam, John Wycliffe and Huss into one voice. It was also the revival of the old conciliar movement which had sought, prematurely as it proved in the event, to subject the papacy to the authority of a General Council. The significance of Luther facing Cajetan and refusing to recant was that this ancient voice had found articulation and would never again be silenced.

5 Luther before Cardinal Cajetan
Contemporary Woodcut

2 Second Hearing: The Leipzig Debate

4–14 July 1519

Trial by debate

The most feared disputant in the German academic world, John Eck, professor of Ingolstadt, and the most vociferous supporter of papal absolutism entered the lists. He was determined to break Luther and emerge as champion of the Pope.

Eck was vulgar, loud-mouthed, coarse, embodying all the vices of the securalized and corrupted ecclesiastics of the time. Protestant theologians and historians have always been hard on Eck, not without cause, but recent Roman Catholic scholarship has rightly set him in a better light showing him to be a scholar in his own right, strong, fearless and independent. This can now be fairly granted.

Yet his whole conduct in his battle with Luther showed him as unscrupulous and double-dealing. He had met Luther when the latter was at Augsburg before Cajetan and had shared amicable exchanges with him on the subject of an open hearing of the Lutheran theology before some university or another. Luther had left it with Eck to suggest by letter a convenient time and place. He heard nothing more of it until he learned that Eck had summoned not Luther but Carlstadt, a senior contemporary of Luther, to debate with him at Leipzig on the subjects of penance, purgatory, indulgences, the papal authority to remit sin, and the primacy of the Pope and the Roman Church. By the latter term Eck meant a divine infallible right instituted by Christ and exercised by the Pope. Eck had cleverly contrived to defeat the Luther theology by vanquishing the Wittenberg faculty in the person of its senior though weakest member and on the very place where John Huss had been condemned a century before.

It was one thing for Eck to challenge Carlstadt, but it was another to do so on the subject of the Lutheran theology. Carlstadt was, for all his brilliance, slow and incompetent in controversy. The result was a foregone conclusion. Everybody knew that it would be academic slaughter, and that Carlstadt would be annihilated with brilliance and sarcasm, a sorry spectacle, but a magnificently colourful and cheap victory over evangelical theology. Luther complained in no uncertain terms of Eck's procedure, a criticism which Eck largely conceded by sending his apologies.

Luther countered by sending his own theses for debate and indicating his intention to be there. Most of the theses are on penitence, indulgences, papal and priestly remission of sin, free will and grace, views we have already analysed. He added a further on papal supremacy round which the debate was to turn. Luther had now behind him some ten years of hard academic study of a critical and historical kind and had thereby put himself in a strong position for an academic debate. He challenged Eck on the papal supremacy, showing it was built on far-fetched decrees and was nothing else than ecclesiastical pretension promulgated during the previous four centuries but contrary to the known historical facts of the first eleven, contrary too to Scripture and Nicaea. Luther boldly asserted his contempt for all the sycophants and flatterers who pretended the matter was different.

Such expressions terrified even his friends and supporters, but even they were not aware of the firm ground on which Luther stood. His early years in the monastery had made him doubt all that his mentors were teaching him about God and the alleged ways of finding and understanding him. Luther found the God of the Christian religion in the Bible and nowhere else. And what he found, or rather found him, was God and nobody else : the God and Father of our Lord, Jesus Christ.

Many of his contemporaries and critics were toying with a figment of their own imagination when they used the term God, and that is why they sat loose to the questionableness of indulgences, papal infallibility and the rest of the ecclesiastical techniques. Not only did he find God but he rediscovered the Gospel and the authority of the Bible. When the papists reacted against his criticism of the hawking of indulgences, refusing to brook any criticism of the Pope or contemporary theology, Luther was driven back to an intensive study of the structure and meaning of the ancient Church as well as the role of the medieval popes. He tackled this problem with all the scientific criticism and intellectual tools of the humanists, and was one of the first to apply historical and linguistic analysis to the study of institutions as well as ideas. In this respect Luther was a modern.

There was a further fact which contributed to Luther's rock-like character. He developed to a high degree the religious reformer's conviction that what he was engaged on was work prompted, guided and sustained by God. He felt himself but a humble instrument in the hand of God. He knew his cause could never fail, even if he did, because God could not fail. Luther's courage was born of a prophetic faith for which the future could be expressed in the past tense.

In preparation for his forthcoming test Luther carefully and critically examined the New Testament, not only for those texts which the papalists claimed supported their view, but the many passages which controverted it. Equally carefully he studied what the Fathers had had to say on the subject of the papacy: Cyprian, Jerome, Augustine, Gregory and others, as well as an examination of the decretals of the early Catholic Councils, Nicaea in particular. Canon Law, too, he examined and pondered in relation to the Bible, the Fathers and Catholic tradition prior to the medieval period. The result of this historical enquiry was a mass of incontrovertible evidence against the prevalent claims of popes, canonists and schoolmen.

All this material Luther assembled in a treatise on papal power to be published if he were unable to take part in the debate. He claims the full and free right to examine the papacy and its claims in the light of the Bible and of historical criticism. He does not invalidate papal decrees as such, but wants to give them their proper role in the church as interpretative or guiding norms. They cannot be considered as infallible, nor as equal to Scripture. To argue that the Pope is inerrant, and to claim that only he can interpret Scripture is to argue against brute historic fact: it is sycophancy and sophistry. Luther saw himself neither as a heretic nor an innovator of novel doctrines: he stood in the full line of Catholic tradition from the Bible through the Fathers. It was his enemies who were the innovators, it was they who were the heretics.

Whatever faults a modern critical historian may find in Luther's statement, quite certainly he will find that Luther submitted all his facts and all his interpretations to plain, historical, critical canons of judgment. None of his opponents did. To find the developed medieval papacy in the New Testament, the Fathers, and in the ancient traditions, as the papists claimed to do, is to fumble with fallacies. To attempt this task with an opponent such as Luther who had pored over the source material with both mind and soul was to court disaster.

It is a shattering thought that Luther's theology should be debated and Luther deliberately excluded from the debate. Yet so it was planned. Hamlet was staged at Leipzig without the prince. The Duke refused point blank to allow Luther to appear unless Eck were to permit it. To this specific request Eck refused to answer. Luther actually went as an attendant of Carlstadt—a deliberate and mean affront. He did not know till he arrived there whether he would even be allowed to speak.

As they entered the town on 24 June 1519 the wheel of Carlstadt's cart broke, throwing him, and his books, in the mud. The crowds thought that a bad omen for the Wittenberg cause. On the same day the bishop of the diocese sought to paralyse the

discussion by issuing his inhibition on the proceedings. Duke
George overruled the mandate, claiming the right of free discussion for his university. The entire theological faculty sided
with Rome against Luther, though he had considerable support
from professors of non-theological subjects.

The first four days were spent in debate on the subject of free
will and grace. Carlstadt was no match for the blustering,
vociferous Eck, playing more for victory than truth, always
with his eye to the gallery. Nevertheless, Eck did not get all his
own way with Carlstadt. Admittedly Eck trounced Carlstadt to
the great delight of the papalists, but a careful reading of the
script shows a deep sincerity of truth in Carlstadt: if the script
alone existed, and no observers' opinions, historians would perhaps award the debate to Carlstadt rather than to Eck.

Interest revived when Luther stepped on to the rostrum on
4 July. Theologians could argue on free will and grace for ever,
could differ over the wide range of metaphysical and scholastic
argument, without ever raising the question of schism or heresy.
So ranged Eck and Carlstadt with their four days of shadow
boxing. But when Luther stepped in to the ring the spectators
knew there would be no punches pulled, that this man would
tackle pragmatic not remote scholastic issues, that this man
would fight, fight to win, and fight to a finish. Luther challenged
the whole matter of authority as it had become embodied in the
papacy and the medieval Church. His opponents believed that
Luther challenged divine authority as embodied in a divine
institution, and had set himself as an apostate to the true faith.
The entire ecclesiastical establishment sought to liquidate him.
Even though many of them agreed with him theologically, they
all sided with established authority, and satisfied their consciences on the grounds of expediency—Luther must be condemned for the sake of the Church. And then there was the
entire lay establishment—kings, rulers, old families, vested
interests, all afraid of revolution, intuitively conservative. Add to
that the immense weight of the unlettered, ignorant peasant

6 The Elector Frederick
the Wise
*Engraving by Lucas
Cranach the Elder*

7 John Eck
*From an anonymous
engraving*

8 Leo X (1513–21) with his nephews Cardinals Medici (later, Pope Clement VII) and Rossi
From the painting by Raphael (Pitti Palace, Florence)

masses. For Luther to take a lone stand against the Church was to declare himself in the wrong, and to forfeit his life and salvation. Even the Emperor was later to mumble, 'Surely one man cannot be right and all the rest wrong?'

It was in this atmosphere that the papalist champion Eck, the representative of the known, accepted establishment, there by divine authority, challenged the lone Luther. Eck began by asserting the divine right and institution of the papal monarchy over a single body, the Church. Luther replied that the statement had no force for him: he too, believed in a universal head of the Church. Eck then claimed that Christ has invested this headship in the Pope as the successor of Peter. This proved that the authority was divine, a claim that could be supported with reference to Cyprian and Jerome. Luther replied, by detailed reference to the New Testament, that the teaching of the entire corpus clearly maintained that Christ, and not a man, was the Head of the Church, and also the foundation, and that other foundation can no man lay than had been laid. Turning to the patristic references Luther showed that Eck had misinterpreted for his own argument what the Fathers had written, for both Cyprian and Jerome had argued that all bishops were successors to the Apostles, and Jerome had pointed out that no distinction was made in the New Testament between the word bishop and presbyter. If one were to argue from historical precedent, the mother of all churches is Jerusalem, not Rome, and as late as Nicaea, the Bishop of Rome was accorded an equality with the bishops of Alexandria and Antioch. At its highest, the Western Fathers regarded Rome and respected her as the principal church in the West. Clear historical evidence indicates that there was no acknowledged divine primacy vested in the Bishop of Rome in the early centuries, no idea of a universal bishop or Pope. Luther here quoted the decrees of the Council of Nicaea, the African Synod of 397, and the letters of Cyprian, the clearest evidence for the equality of bishops in the ancient Church. Further, the Eastern Church had never recognized any idea of

E

a Roman primacy. Here was open historical criticism at work for the first time. The evidence of the New Testament and the evidence of history showed the folly of Eck's attempt to defend the idea of the divine right of papal primacy on the foundation of the New Testament and on the basis of historical precedent.

Eck appealed to St Bernard in support of his point of the necessity of a head of the Church on earth. He also sought to refute Luther's scriptural exegesis, and to controvert his deployment of Cyprian and Jerome. History, he argued, has shown how all the churches to which Luther referred, Jerusalem, Antioch and Alexandria, were contaminated by heresy and had gone under: Rome alone, founded on the rock against which the gates of hell should never prevail, had never foundered, but had preserved the truth intact and uncorrupted. In the same way, as Christ is the Head of the church triumphant, so the Pope, His Vicar, the successor of Peter, is the head of the church militant. This is clear evidence that it is not by human right but by divine right that the Pope rules in Rome. The evidence of the Greek Church does not affect this claim: the Greeks are, in fact, exiles. True, there may have been no such title as the universal bishop, but it does not alter the fact that that is how the Pope was recognized in practice.

In reply to evidence from the Fathers in support of the divine right of the papacy, Luther adduced Scripture. He venerated the Fathers, but set the Word of God above the word of man. Yet even here, there were canons of criticism: scripture was to be interpreted in its own light, the genuine, specific meaning of the passage. Here Luther showed himself the critical, scientific, linguistic scholar. In the New Testament all the apostles were equal. Peter had no primacy and no authority over the other apostles: he was first, but his prerogative was one of honour not power. A primacy of honour Luther was willing to grant the Pope, but not one of power. Never divine authority, never infallibility.

Eck rejoined that Scripture explicitly taught that Christ

founded His Church on Peter the rock (Matt. 16.18). Peter had
been instituted by divine authority as monarch of the church, a
power Peter had bestowed upon his successors. This divine
authority was an essential ingredient of the whole idea of the
unity of the Church, and indeed had been instituted by Christ
to this end. To this view Eck adduced opinions from Jerome,
Ambrose and Augustine.

Luther countered by holding that Christ was the foundation
of the Church incontrovertibly, and that whatever the meaning
of the metaphor 'rock', the foundation clearly meant Christ or
faith in Christ. Further, it was a dark error to equate the word
Church on Christ's lips with the Roman Church as Eck did. The
word Church meant the people of God generally, not the Roman
communion. Here Luther reiterated an important distinction
which Rome refused to countenance. Luther was never against
the Church: to him it was part of the Gospel, but his exegetical
and historical analysis understood the Church in the biblical sense
of the called people of God, largely within the institution but
never coterminous. Luther believed in the Catholic Church, the
universal People of God, called of God and known of God, but
would never equate this idea with the Roman Church. To Luther
Scripture was its own interpreter, and to him it was clear as day
that the total witness of the New Testament affirmed that
Christ and Christ only was the head and the foundation of the
Church. Even if Eck could claim some kind of support from
Augustine and the later Fathers for his interpretation, there
was no doubt whatsoever that as authorities they must take second
place to the plain words of Peter himself, 'To whom coming
as unto a living stone, disallowed indeed of men, but chosen of
God, and precious' (I Peter 2.4), and of Paul, 'For other foundation can no man lay than that is laid, which is Jesus Christ'
(I Cor. 3.11), both of whom clearly taught that Christ Himself
is the foundation on which the Church is built. Moreover, the
main weight of patristic evidence clearly supported the New Testament evidence. Again Luther shines as the modern scholar: not

a mere reference to an authority can clinch an argument, but the weighing and estimating of the authority itself in relation to other authorities. Luther further added, that the historical evidence incontrovertibly witnesses that the ancient Eastern Church had never acknowledged the primacy of Rome; that the Church of the East had existed long before Rome; that its long line of bishops had existed without reference to Rome. Does Eck, Luther asked, regard this church as outside the Church, and its martyrs, its saints, its theologians? Does Eck want to dismiss a saint, scholar and theologian of the stature of Gregory Nazianzus, to take but one example, as a heretic? A schismatic? A Hussite?

Eck was cornered and had to withdraw his earlier sweeping condemnation of the Church of the East. But, with the energy of a cornered animal, he darted from the defence of an untenable position to the attack. In denying the papal primacy as of divine right, Eck declared, Luther was merely defending the views of Marsiglio, Wiclif and Huss, views firmly and clearly condemned by the Church. Luther was merely a champion of the Bohemians, who, he slyly added, had already claimed Luther their new hero. By this remark Eck made a direct appeal to the prejudices of his audience. It was in Leipzig that Huss was condemned. The university itself was founded in 1409 owing to the religious and racial conflicts between the Germans and the Czechs, when all the Germans withdrew from Prague to Leipzig. Of all places Leipzig was sensitively anti-Hussite.

Luther at first parried this as irrelevant, but in the resumed debate Luther openly asserted that among the articles of Huss, which had been unjustly condemned by Rome, many were both Christian and evangelical. This remark created an uproar. Duke George exploded and swore loudly, 'A plague on the man!' Luther continued to substantiate his point. He gave the Hussite view which argued that it was not necessary to salvation to believe that the Roman Church was superior to all other Churches. Hussite or Wycliffite, nevertheless many Greek Fathers and bishops who were saved, Basil the Great, Gregory of

Nazianzus, Epiphanius, did not hold this article of belief. Neither Pope nor Inquisitor had right or authority to add new articles of faith. Nor could any man be compelled to believe extra-biblical teaching. The Roman supremacy may be accepted on the grounds of religious reverence, or as a practical arrangement to avoid schism. But it was another matter to argue divine authority and utterly unacceptable to condemn the holy men who had not accepted it.

Eck wanted to know why Luther was using all his skill and scholarship to attack the Holy Father. Why not employ it against the heretics? Luther, he argued, was defending the heretics under the guise of defending the Greek Fathers. He persisted that Luther was a Hussite. He maintained that Luther was defending certain Hussite teachings against the decisions of a General Council, Constance. To question the authority of a Council was to make all Council decisions open to question. As far as Eck was concerned, to question a matter clearly pronounced by either Pope or Council, was heretical *in eo ipso*.

Luther objected to the bandying about of such opprobrious epithets as 'heretical'. A matter of heresy should be adjudged by appropriate authority, not in a slanging match on 'pestilential articles'. Of these latter, Luther instanced several that were both sound and Catholic, held not only by Luther, but by Augustine and Peter Lombard, even Eck himself. The charge of heresy, therefore, could equally be levelled at Eck! The Council had actually declared only some of the articles to be heretical, others were erroneous, rash or offensive. All these charges had been levelled at Christ. To argue as Eck had done that to question a decision of any Council is to endanger its authority, in support of such a contention, and to lead in Augustine, was to adduce a false authority. Augustine was referring to infallible Scripture not fallible Councils. Pope and Council are all alike men, subject to the apostolic injunction to prove all things and to hold fast to the good (I Thess. 5.21). Canonists shared Luther's view that a Council may err.

Eck knew the entire audience was on his side, and a view so dangerous as the errancy of Councils could be deployed to his own advantage. Luther's views on the fallibility of Councils had already created an uproar in the hall. Eck largely and roundly declared as an infallible dogma that whatever a Council (legitimately called) defined or determined on matters of faith, was absolutely final and certain. It was abominable for Luther to opine that because a Council was composed of men its decisions were simply human, for a Council was ruled not by men but by God.

Luther knew the weight of the prejudice now rising against him, and was astute enough to sense that it was originating not in the content of the discussion, which many of his hearers could neither follow nor grasp, but was being built up on ignorance and rumour. He asked the court if he could be allowed to address them in German. He then explained to them in their mother tongue the odious nature of the contrived insinuation that he was Hussite and therefore a heretic. Further, he had no interest in dissuading people from obedience to Rome, nor did he seek to impugn the Roman primacy. He wanted to make it clear that to believe primacy was not a divine right, did not effect a man's loyalty to the papacy. He knew that obedience to the papacy was not scriptural dogma, but that did not mean he did not recognize the normal need for dutiful obedience to the Pope. In a general way he accepted the decrees of the Councils, but it was another matter to claim they were inerrant. Certainly no Council or Pope could establish new dogma. The onus was on Eck to prove that a Council has never erred and can never err: a Council by its very nature cannot have divine right ascribed to its promulgations. To this Eck had no reply except to say that if anybody said that a Council erred or can err, let him be as a heathen and publican.

For the remaining days of the debate (9–14 July) the subjects ranged over purgatory, indulgences, penance and absolution. Luther showed himself prepared to concede the feasibility of the doctrine of purgatory, but would not concede it as scriptural doctrine. On the matter of indulgences Eck went all the way with Luther. Eck sought neither to defend the indulgence preachers, nor the scandal of the traffic that had grown up with the idea. To him indulgences were neither necessary nor obligatory, though he showed himself prepared to accept the matter as an ecclesiastical institution. He further defended the power of the Pope to grant remission to a penitent, and believed that such remission should not be limited merely to penitential works. Luther was later to say that the storm would never have arisen had the Church practised Eck's teaching on the matter of indulgences. There was not the same agreement when the two disputants discussed the scriptural teaching on penance and absolution. To Luther Eck got as deep into the Scriptures as a water spider into water: he flees from them like the Devil flees the Cross. Luther declared of himself that he duly reverenced the Fathers but preferred the authority of Scriptures: they would be the future judges of the debate. Sourly Eck retorted that Luther was scurrilous and did not wear the gravity becoming a theologian. Luther seemed to want to set himself up as a kind of Delphic oracle with an understanding of the Scriptures greater than any Father.

The Debate Assessed

Both men showed learning of such a kind as to outstrip the thinking of the Leipzig theologians, who found the debate very tough going. The disputation suffered from a rather tedious analysis of arguments repetitiously handled, too much detail, too many fine points, and an endless weight of references to canon law and church history as well as the Bible. Eck was as ready as he was able, and nobody in Germany, perhaps Christendom, could match him for his oratorical skill and learning. He knew perhaps more canon law than Luther, was a little less knowledgeable on patristics, but no match for Luther in biblical learning. On this last ground, Luther towered peerless in Christendom.

The real difference between the men lies in the fact that Eck used all his authorities, Bible, history, tradition, usage and so on, to buttress and support what he already believed on *a priori* dogmatic assumptions. Luther, on the other hand, was a pioneer of modern linguistic and historical criticism, who faced every question as an open question, who examined all his sources, not only in the exact meaning of the words, but in their own original setting. (This ability further develops over the next few months.) When Eck began to realize he was after all not universally acknowledged as the victor but on the contrary incurred some telling criticisms from responsible quarters (indicated below), he undertook to prosecute his campaign in Rome. He took with him some of Luther's writings and his own *magnum opus, On Papal Primacy—against Luther*. This work was based on the writings of Pseudo-Dionysius, on the forged Papal Decretals, on the interpolated canons of Nicaea, and on other fallacious documents. He himself said the work earned high praise of the Pope. The crucial point is that he and his partisans were so alien to Luther's rational and historical critique. Eck championed the old world—truth by authoritative declaration: Luther the new—truth by open and responsible examination. There was a further profound difference. Luther had started out on his search as a disillusioned and disappointed critic, who had found out that the god's feet were made of clay. He had seen through the scandal of indulgences and the buying and selling of Christ conducted in the interests of a secularized Church and a corrupt society. He had broken through into the meaning of the Bible, and had learned Greek and Hebrew to understand it fully. For years now he had studied the Fathers, not in selected catenae, but in their context, and had added an immense knowledge of Church history. Above all, his critical faculty had exfoliated in a burning experience of God in Christ, and he now knew no peace of mind until every historical, intellectual and spiritual issue was resolved by this touchstone. Into this kingdom Eck never entered: he was not even aware of it when a citizen from that land faced him on the rostrum. Because Luther was a man of the new learning, and Eck merely reasserted more bluntly, or more cleverly, the old position which was not open to debate, Luther's second hearing was indeterminative. The divine dimension, of getting to grips with a man mastered by God, was never approached in the debate.

Most of the witnesses, impressed by bombast and manner rather than truth and content, who in any event were prejudiced in favour of the old against the uncertainty of the new, believed that Eck had dealt a crushing blow to the Wittenbergers. To a few it was clear that he never actually met the arguments of the reformers. It was not unnoticed that in character and demeanour he fell far short of the purity and sincerity of the learned Carlstadt, of the earnestness and fire of Luther, and of the theological acuity of the shy young Melanchthon sitting at the side taking notes. When the hearing was over Eck wrote bombastically to the world at large of his triumph. He dismissed Melanchthon as 'that little grammatist'. He engaged on a further debate at the university and 'slaughtered' another opponent. The Leipzig faculty made the most of their visiting professor. He was feted and feasted right royally. Not for him the common Leipzig beer which was much too plebeian: more to his sophisticated taste the city's 'wine and voluptuous prostitutes'. Like all the papalists, from the Pope down, Eck never understood the truth and urgency of the issues raised by Luther, the scholarly, God-consumed monk. Unlike Eck, Luther returned home at once, quiet, thoughtful, disappointed : he wanted to work, to think, to pray. Certain neutral observers and thoughtful laymen were aware that the debate had not gone to Eck after all. They began to notice truth seeping up through the cracks. As one expressed it, only the learned saw the truth of the Wittenberg argument; the rest who applauded Eck were as fit to judge the issues as a donkey to play a harp.

Eventually, time set the debate in a truer perspective. Eck began to find that everybody was not on his side after all. Melanchthon wrote a devastating criticism in reply to Eck's attack on him as a 'little grammatist'. The scholars and humanists were entirely with Melanchthon here and against Eck. Oecolampadius, the Swiss reformer, dealt Eck a crushing attack. A humanist poet poked fun at him. Angered, he pressed his university to have a public burning of all the Wittenberg books, but the old scholar Reuchlin scotched such unseemly retaliation as unworthy of a university. The universities of Paris and Erfurt (which the disputants had mutually agreed would be the official judges of the debate) withdrew their support of Eck, only Louvain and Cologne, (both in the hands of the Inquisitor), held out against Luther. Certainly the judgment of the academic world was non-committal, a sign of the times not noticed by the papalists.

The hearing at Leipzig at least clarified the issues. Luther now fully realized, a fact pointed out by Cajetan a year earlier but now appreciated increasingly by Germany, that his first attack on the scandalous traffic in indulgences was now a matter of dead history. No longer was Luther dealing with a mere abuse of a rather harmless ecclesiastical discipline, but with the entire theological structure and spiritual practice of Christianity. Beyond the errors of indulgences, beyond the theological figments of purgatory and the treasury of merits, supported as they were by the unformulated ideas of the mediatorial power of the priesthood and the infallible authority of the papacy, Luther had travelled into the new world of critical biblical scholarship and the humanistic examination of historical sources. He had in fact now struck a dagger at the heart of Catholic Christendom as it then understood itself. He had gained the right, and the responsibility, of every individual man to see for himself and to think for himself, to follow the argument where it leads. Luther now made it plain for the first time that he utterly denied the divine origin, the divine right, and the divine authority of the papacy. He further denied the total unquestioning infallibility of a Council and its decrees. As a seat of pastoral and spiritual authority necessary to the guidance of Christendom Luther had no objections to the papacy as such, but every objection to it as a secularized authority claiming infallibility and divine right unquestionably over all christians. He further showed appropriate respect for the decrees of councils, arguing that they were subject to all informed and critical enquiry, never to be classed as infallible and beyond question. His basic authority he laid on the Word and Work of God as recorded in the Bible. All men, even the Church, were under the Bible: no man, not even the Church, could set itself above the Bible. At this point, the twentieth century word 'fundamentalist' should not be used of Luther. He did not equate the word of the Bible with the Word of God: the word of the Bible contained the Word of God, and expressed God's Word, but Luther deployed, for his day, the most exact literary, historical, linguistic and textual criticism on the Scriptures. Such an authority, for Luther, demanded responsible, private judgment. It never meant, as critics foolishly decry, the setting up of one's own private judgment against the weight of appropriate academic authority, ecclesiastical authority and the weight of history and tradition but rather, the responsibility of every man to appropriate truth to himself by sound thinking. As well as Scripture and responsible judgment, Luther held the necessity of faith, not in the sense of a corpus of beliefs to be held, nor yet as a kind of psychological approach that man contributes in relation to God, but in the sense that he has nothing at all to contribute and that the work of God is the kindling of this divine spark in the mind and soul of man.

It amounts to a revolution, a new kind of enquiry, where the evidence is not what man believes, thinks or does but rather a submission to what God has done and is doing in the contemporary scene. It is not faith in man's beliefs, in man's formulation of doctrine, in man's formulation of spiritual practice. It is in fact a deliverance from that altogether into a submission to a critical examination of what God did in recorded history and is actually doing in the confused welter of activities of secularized princes, power-drunk ecclesiastics and desperate peasants all claiming the centre of the picture. Faith in Luther's mind meant the turning of his back on all such futile anthropocentricities and the turning of his mind to what was a hidden but active God.

With this kind of faith there went a trust or confidence both in God and in the environment He had created, wrecked as it virtually was by a creation determined on its own way, determined to get all it could as long as it could, locked in the captivity of its own self-interest. Luther believed in God, believed God would prevail, believed God had called him out of the empty, self-created human chaos into a larger room, a larger purpose. Like Calvin Luther was totally God-mastered, totally God-centred. Further, Luther's faith carried within it the pulse of hope, for he knew, fail though he may, divided though Christendom might be, in the long run, the only run that mattered, at the end God would not fail and would acknowledge those he knew as victors, even though the world had persecuted them, burned them, crucified them.

This may be described as a 'spiritual Copernican revolution'. Luther's opponents, to continue the analogy, were 'pre-Copernican'. Their theology, as handed down and interpreted and expounded in the tradition, was in their estimation infallible, and therefore final and unchallengeable. They were prisoners of their own traditions, of their own interpretations and anthropocentricisms. Truth was what they thought it to be. Luther on the other hand was 'post-Copernican'. Truth to him was reality as it is, as God had created it and as God was maintaining it. Luther was delivered from the subjectivity of a man seeking God to the objectivity of a man whom God had found. The subjectivity consisted in subjection to the *a priori* authority of the Church: the objectivity in the release from this authority to that liberation found in submitting all *a priori* statements to the *a fortiori* empirical evidence of a man's experience of God in faith by believing in Him and learning of Him from His handling of men and history.

This doctrine of faith effected a revolution in Christendom and became known as Luther's doctrine of justification by faith alone. It was really the fundamental issue between him and his opponents.

In other words, man can offer nothing and do nothing that can make him merit God, he can only allow God to show him his unworthiness and to let Him create him in love, in mercy, and in grace. Man can never justify himself to God, by spiritual effort, intellectual attainment or meritorious works: all is of the sovereign grace and mercy of God. That is what Luther meant by justification by faith, a doctrine he found written on every page of the Bible. These three authorities, Bible, faith and responsible judgment, were all to be attested by sound, open, rational, historical, communicable, informed judgment.

There was one further sequel to the disputation: a violent pamphleteering war broke out with all the verve and colour of sixteenth century language and imagery. Emser, Dungersheim, Rubeus, von Hoogstraten the Inquisitor-General, the theologians of Louvain and Cologne, Alveld, Prierias, the Bishops of Brandenberg and Meissen, all supported Eck and the *status quo*, some offensively, others normally. Oecolampadius, Spengler, Adelmann the canon of Augsburg, Pirkheimer, Pellican, Bucer, Capito, Montanus, Museus, Crotus Rubianus, and Ulrich von Hutten all joined in the battle on Luther's side. And, of course, none was more effective, none could be more devastating with words and pictures than Martin himself. The humanists were delighted to see these pompous reactionaries rolled in the mud, the sport of village youth. Many a high person suddenly found himself the butt of robust Nordic humour which made even his friends laugh.

Armchair critics four and a half centuries later find fault with Luther, whom they describe as opinionated, headstrong, violent, obstinate. They would do well to remember that he had to be, if he were to stand the fray. He was engaged in a desperate struggle to maintain single-handed his individual convictions against an overwhelming power which admitted no place for individual conviction, and had only one remedy to deal with it, the dungeon and the stake. Luther in fact guarded his house successfully and handed it on to his heirs. If the bulldog drew a little blood, he had to be commended for keeping the intruders at bay. Could any other dog have succeeded?

Yet there is more to Luther's persistent and aggressive polemic than the psychologist knows. Beyond it was the strength, already alluded to, of an invincible belief that it was God's cause on which he was engaged, to which he had been called, and the outcome of which God would bring to its proper end in His good time. He knew that Eck and the others were equally convinced that they were standing for what was right, but he knew, as they did not, on grounds of critical scholarship, how weak their cause was, how human, how frail their advocacy. He knew God would prevail. He sought the truth, the whole truth, and nothing but the truth. The sum total of all this pamphleteering was to make Luther see himself more clearly and to become aware of the task before him. As it was once finely expressed, the ship of Reformation was on the high seas and Luther found himself at the helm.

The justification of making this disputation a second preliminary hearing of Luther's case lies just there. He was subject to intense examination and cross-examination by a papalist theologian, and out of that hearing emerged more clearly the issues involved. Luther now saw that Christendom was about to be divided and that, what the world came later to call the Reformation, had begun. There remained only one more final hearing, the outcome of which he awaited in confidence and hope.

3 The Pope's Condemnation

It will be recalled (p. 55) that the official Roman prosecution of Luther was held up in the early part of 1519 by diplomatic overtures to Frederick the Wise. These manoeuvres, which carried assurances of a cardinal's hat and a rich bishopric for Luther and the coveted Golden Rose for the prince, were thinly veiled blandishments proferred in the hope of preventing Charles' election as Emperor. When the sober fact of the inevitability of the election of Charles was accepted at Rome these schemes collapsed. Nevertheless, Cajetan still sought to extort from Frederick the repression of Luther, but when it was realized that he would never succeed, he was made the scapegoat of the papal diplomatic failure, fell into disfavour, and left Germany for Italy.

At this stage Cardinal von Miltitz, a young Saxon nobleman attached to the Curia, began further mediatorial efforts to secure Luther's submission to the Pope. To this end he invited Luther to Koblenz in May 1519, to meet the Archbishop of Trier and Cajetan as arbiters, but Luther would have no further dealings with Cajetan after his experience at Augsburg, and thought it the height of folly 'to walk into the lions' den at Koblenz', to use his own words. In September Miltitz finally delivered the Golden Rose (but no cardinal's hat) and with the delivery procured the authority from Frederick to negotiate with his professor. None of the Wittenbergers, not even the Prince, had any confidence in Miltitz, and the meeting, held in Liebenwerda on 9 October, proved abortive in the event.

The Curia now decided to take action. Luther was provided with inside information of this new turn of events from a former fellow student, Crotus Rubianus, now in Italy. His testimony is important and revealing.* He informed Luther that his name was a bad word in Rome, and even to approve his writings was to be guilty of heresy. He said that he had received a copy of the *Ninety-five Theses,* the *Resolutions* in explanation of them, as well as a copy of the *Acta Augustana,* but he dared not admit that openly and could only read them in secret. He went on to say that there were Italian theologians in agreement with Luther but that they were terrified to say so in public, not so much from fear of the Pope, but for the imperative need of maintaining the strength of the papacy at the present juncture. Everybody in Rome, even if they agreed with Luther, felt it of prior importance to maintain that the Pope was the Vicar of Christ, the infallible organ of the Holy Spirit rather than admit any truth in Luther's arguments or evidence. There was no sense in arguing to the contrary, no point even in quoting the Bible, he averred. A hundred Pauls in Rome would not persuade them to give up their false opinions. At Rome the ultimate and only arbiter was the Pope. There was no point even in referring to the patent misrule of the Curia, to its obvious immorality, to its manifest oppression of the innocent. The Dominicans argue that God had ordered it so, and no man may dispute the Will of God. The state of things in Rome was now so bad that a man who was a genuine Christian or a theologian was held in utter contempt. He had witnessed with his own eyes the host carried about with the processional support of bad women and boy prostitutes. He went on to say that what had angered the Medicis (the money-minded relatives and parasites of the papal court) more than anything else about Luther was his appeal for a General Council : these men were determined to maintain the *status quo,* to uphold what they called 'the liberties of the Church' (a euphemism for freedom to exploit

* WBr. 1. 540–4. 16 October 1519.

Christendom), and turned a deaf ear to the cry for reform. He hoped Luther would continue in his struggle and convert Germany to his cause. He doubted the value of further controversial debate with men like Eck.

A fortnight later (31 October 1519)* Rubianus returned to the subject of Eck. He informs Luther that Rome was of the opinion that Eck was the victor at Leipzig and that it had now determined to pursue its course against Luther and the Hussites (*sic*!). Rubianus says he had knowledge through a court physician that Eck had written to the Pope, and that this letter stirred His Holiness to consult privately and urgently two of his theologians. In his letter Eck had given an account of the Leipzig Disputation and had urged the importance of making an immediate example of Luther. If the Pope did not act at once, Saxony would be lost to Christendom, to start a process that would spread throughout Germany. Eck suggested practical steps and advised strong action to silence the humanists, whose biting wit, he said, showed how far the Lutheran disease had spread. Eck advised the Pope to compel the Universities of Erfurt and Paris, official adjudicators of the disputation, to clear the air and pronounce forthwith in favour of Eck. He also further counselled the Pope to appoint a commission to draw up the official condemnation of the Lutheran heresy.

As a result a strong letter was despatched from Rome to Frederick expressing the Pope's displeasure at the long delay in suppressing Luther. The Pope announced his intention of taking strong measures against the movement, including an interdict on Saxony and a ban on Luther. Frederick replied in a hurt tone of justification. He had acted as a Christian prince, he claimed, and as a loyal son of the Church. Miltitz himself had approved of Frederick's plan not to banish Luther so as to contain the problem within the confines of Saxony. Luther had not broken his agreement to keep silent, but had been compelled to speak in order to vindicate himself against subse-

* WBr. 1. 545–6.

F

quent attacks. Further, many learned men approved of Luther's teaching, and were of the view that it could be held without detriment to the Church. The matter was currently being considered of taking the case to the Archbishop of Trier, or even to the next Diet : the Luther affair was, therefore, technically *sub judice*. What had he done, the Elector asked, that he and his dominions should be subjected to an interdict? Frederick was obviously playing to protect his professor, and though Luther treated this kind of diplomacy with short shrift, nevertheless the prince, as prince, was right in shielding Luther, and essentially right to keep negotiations open in diplomatic channels in the way he did.

The Pope and his advisers were not unaware of the meaning of such evasive words, and interpreted this letter for what it was, a bland assertion of respectful disobedience and contumacy. The letter earned for Frederick a public denunciation in Rome on 11 January 1520 as an enemy of the faith and traducer of his people: Luther's repression was demanded. The Pope sent a warning to Frederick through Serralonga notifying him of this public condemnation.

The process against Luther was resumed. A commission, comprising Cajetan, Accolti and the mendicant orders, was appointed, to make a formal investigation of Luther's teaching and to formulate a list of heresies taught by Luther. The two cardinals were competent to engage on such an investigation but the monks were totally inadequate. Eventually, on Cajetan's advice, the commission was reconstituted on 11 February 1520, when the mendicants were left off and a new group of theologians appointed, Prierias and Rhadino* being among the members.

Under Cajetan's guidance an intelligent, conciliatory attitude was taken. Luther's writings were read and discussed by the commission, and a real effort made to understand them and not to condemn them outright without discriminating what

* *Alias* Dr. Emser (1477–1527), secretary of Duke George and a bitter literary opponent of Luther.

might properly be termed heretical, and what merely scandalous or offensive. A moderate line was taken which, whilst rejecting Luther's theology without mentioning him by name, offered a chance to retract before taking the final step of condemnation. Cajetan considered it of extreme importance not to disrupt the Church. A final appeal was made to Staupitz to persuade Luther to submit and to stop afflicting the poor, long-suffering Pope, to cease to undermine the rock on which the Lord had founded the Church. A Bull was now in actual preparation, though the Pope wanted to give Luther one last chance to come to his senses.

This approach represented Cajetan's intelligent and reasonable attitude rather than the Pope's. In the meantime the latter had been listening to Eck, who revealed the cataclysmic nature of Luther's attack on the papacy, the power of which had not been fully realized by the Church. The Pope at once appointed another commission more to his liking, comprising Eck, two cardinals and a Spanish divine. This commission drew up a list of 41 errors in the form of a condemnatory Bull, to be brought before the Consistory. Four meetings were held between 21 May and 1 June. The Bull was finally drawn up making no distinction in Luther's views, but condemning them *in toto* as heretical. Cajetan's views and advice were disregarded. The Bull was publicly proclaimed on 15 June 1520, the occasion being enlivened by a bonfire of Luther's works in the Piazza Navona, just to demonstrate how serious Rome felt about the whole business.

Summary of the Bull, 'Exsurge Domine' 15 June 1520

The title page of the Bull, which is some 30 pages of text, reads *Bull against the errors of Martin Luther and his followers.*

In the prelude the Pope invokes God, St Peter, St Paul, all saints and finally the Church, declaring to them how a wild boar had entered the vineyard [a fatuous attempt to be relevant since at the moment of issue he was at his hunting lodge hunting wild boar]. This wild beast was ravishing the Church and must be put down, for he actually attacks the popes and their teachings.

Luther and his followers simply revive the errors of the Greeks and the Bohemians, views long since condemned by authority. Their writings, where not heretical, are erroneous, scandalous, offensive or misleading. Such men are agents of Satan, even though they stem from the race which has been the guardian of the Holy Roman Empire.

The Pope then listed a selection of 41 errors culled from Luther's writings, a collection which bears all the marks of superficiality and haste.

1 It is an heretical opinion, even if it is commonly held, that the sacraments of the New Testament grant justifying grace so long as a man does not set up an obstacle.

2 To say that sin does not abide in a child after baptism is to condemn both Christ and Paul at one and the same time.

3 The tinder of sin, even though there be no actual commission of sin, hinders a soul departing the body from entrance into heaven.

4 Imperfect love necessarily brings with it a great dread to a man facing death, which in itself alone is enough to create the pains of purgatory and impede his entry into heaven.

5 The statement that there are three parts to penance : contrition, confession and satisfaction, has no foundation in Holy Scripture nor in the ancient holy Christian doctors.

6 A contrition, processed by means of the discussion, accumulation and detestation of sins, whereby a man thinks over his past years in bitterness of soul, by weighing the seriousness of his sins, their multitude and their repulsiveness, the loss of eternal blessedness and the gaining of eternal damnation, a contrition of this kind breeds hypocrisy, in fact it breeds a sinner, which is worse.

7 Very true is the proverb and better by far than any doctrine of contrition taught up till now: 'The supreme penitence is to sin no more.' 'A new life is the greatest repentance' (In the original, WA. 1. 321. 2–6, Luther supports this by quoting Gal. 6.15. 'In Christ neither circumcision nor uncircumcision avails anything, but a new creature'.)

8 You must in no way presume to confess all venial sins, nor for that matter all mortal sins, for it is impossible to know all one's mortal sins. For this reason they used to confess only the manifest mortal sins in the primitive Church.

9 In that we want to confess all our sins completely, we are doing nothing else than to want to leave nothing to be forgiven by the mercy of God.

10 Sins are not remitted to him who does not believe they are remitted to him personally when a priest gives absolution. Indeed the sin would remain unless he believe it had been forgiven. The remission of the sin and the gift of grace are not sufficient in themselves: a man has to believe that he has been forgiven.

11 You must on no account believe that you have been absolved on account of your own contrition, but on account of the word of Christ, 'Whatsoever sins you remit they are remitted'. Thus, I say, when you have obtained the absolution of a priest, believe with all your heart that you have been absolved. This is true absolution, whatever else there might be in the way of contrition.

12 If it were possible for a man to make his confession yet not be contrite; or if a priest were to absolve him jestingly; yet, if in spite of this he believes himself to have been absolved, most truly is he absolved.

13 In the sacrament of penance and the remission of guilt the Pope or bishop effects no more than the humblest priest; indeed, where there is no priest, any Christian whatsoever, even a woman or a child, may equally do as much.

14 No one is obliged to say to the priest that he is contrite, nor ought the priest to require that of the penitent.

15 Great is the error of those who go to the sacrament of the Eucharist relying on the fact that they have been to confession, that they are not conscious of any mortal sin whatever; that they have sent on ahead their prayers and preparations. These all eat and drink judgment to themselves. If on the contrary they believe and trust that they will receive grace at the Eucharist then it is this faith alone that makes them pure and worthy.

16 It seems to have been decided that the Church in common council established that the laity should communicate in both kinds; the Bohemians who communicate in both kinds are not heretics but schismatics.

17 The treasures of the Church, from which the Pope grants indulgences, are not the merits of Christ and the saints.

18 Indulgences are pious frauds practised upon the faithful; they are remissions from good works and belong to those things which may be permitted but not to those things which are profitable.

19 Indulgences, for those who genuinely gain them are of no avail for the remission of punishment which is owing to God for actual sins committed.

20 People who believe that indulgences are salutary and useful in bringing forth the fruits of the Spirit are deceived.

21 Indulgences are necessary only for public crimes and may properly be granted only for hard cases and for the undisciplined.

22 For six classes of men indulgences are neither necessary nor useful : namely, for the dead and those at point of death; the infirm; those reasonably let or hindered; those who have not committed crimes; those who have committed crimes but not public ones; those who devote themselves to better things.

23 Excommunication is only an external penalty, and does not

deprive a man of the common spiritual prayers of the Church.

24 Christians must be taught to love excommunication rather than fear it.

25 The Roman Pontiff, successor to Peter, is not the Vicar of Christ over all the churches of the world, instituted by Christ Himself in the person of blessed Peter.

26 The saying of Christ to Peter, 'Whatsoever thou shalt bind on earth shall be bound in heaven' applies only to those things bound by Peter himself.

27 It is certain that it is not in the power of the Church or the Pope to go ahead and establish articles of faith nor, for that matter, laws concerning morals or good works.

28 If the Pope with a great part of the Church thought so-and-so, even though he did not err, it is still not a sin or a heresy to think otherwise, especially in a matter not necessary for salvation, until such time one alternative is condemned or another is approved by General Council.

29 A way has been opened up to us of checking the authority of Councils, and of freely contradicting their proceedings and judging their decrees, and of confidently confessing whatever seems true, whether approved or condemned by any Council whatever.

30 Some articles of John Huss condemned at the Council of Constance are most Christian, utterly true and evangelical; these the whole Catholic Church could not condemn.

31 In every good work the righteous man sins.

32 A good work done with the best intentions is still a venial sin.

33 To burn heretics is against the will of the Spirit.

34 To go to war against the Turks is to fight against God as He visits our iniquities upon us through them.

35 No one is certain that he is not always sinning mortally on account of the deeply hidden sin of pride.

36 Free will after sin is a matter only of words, and a man sins mortally even as long as he does what in him lies.

37 Purgatory cannot be proved from Holy Scripture, at least, canonical Scripture.

38 Souls in purgatory are not certain of their salvation, at any rate not all of them. Neither can it be proved by any argument or any scripture that these souls are beyond the state of acquiring merit or of growing in love.

39 Souls in purgatory sin without intermission as long as they seek peace and dread punishments.

40 Souls freed from purgatory by the prayers of the living are less blessed than if they had completed the satisfactions on their own.

41 Ecclesiastical prelates and secular princes would not do a bad thing if they destroyed all the begging bags of the mendicants.

The Pope then describes these propositions *en bloc* as heretical, scandalous, offensive and contrary to Catholic truth: they seduce the minds of the faithful and run counter to charity and obedience. They are contrary to the teaching and traditions of the Catholic Church. They argue that the Church may err, a view contrary to the teaching of the Fathers, the canons of Councils, and the papal decretals. All the views expressed are disapproved, condemned and rejected.

The Pope then decrees that the defence of these errors or the publication of them is forthwith prohibited to clergy and laity alike under pain of inhibition, excommunication, disqualification and the confiscation of every tenure. Such people, if they disobey, will be refused Christian burial and be disqualified from all legal proceedings: they will incur the charge of infamous conduct, treachery, treason, heresy and harbouring heretics. Here follows an exhaustive list of persons to whom these strictures apply: all and every cleric from archbishop and cardinal down to the meanest priest and monk; emperors, kings, nobility, judges, soldiers and the rest, including the humble householder; all places were to be included, all communities, including universities.

All of Luther's writings are forbidden to everybody to read, possess or defend: the bishops are to seek them out and burn them publicly.

The Pope avers that all that could be done to save Luther had been done. He had sought as a father to invite him to Rome at his own expense so that he could restore his wayward son. Luther refuses to listen and goes from bad to worse. The Pope has every power of canon law to proceed against Luther as a notorious heretic, yet still makes one last effort to persuade Luther to repent and return to the fold, when he would receive the same welcome as did the Prodigal Son of the parable.

Luther is suspended from the functions of the ministry. He may no longer write, teach or publish. He is given 60 days to recant. His books must be burnt publicly. Luther himself must make a public and legal recantation. Or still better, come to Rome and do the same. Failure to do so by Luther and his followers will incur the charge of notorious and stubborn heretics, and proceedings will be taken against them according to law.

No Catholic may read, print, publish or defend any book of Luther written or to be written, whether tacitly or expressly. All such books are to be burned. After the excommunication, all Christian people are forbidden to hold any intercourse with Luther and his followers, or to give them shelter, on pain of interdict. Magistrates are commanded to arrest all such people and send them to Rome. No man may have any commerce with such people, nor any kind of fellowship or friendship: they are to be denied the necessaries of life.

All Christian people have the right to arrest Luther personally, as well as any of his followers, supporters and harbourers, hold them in custody and deliver them to Rome. Any place which harbours Luther and his supporters is subject to the interdict.

Readers will note that the Bull condemns Luther's writings

and teachings outright but does not in fact excommunicate Luther himself. It contains the 'evangelical monition', an opportunity for him to repent and retract. Excommunication was to depend only in the event of his refusal to retract. Excommunication actually took place six months later by the Bull *Decet Romanum,* 3 January 1521 (see p. 96). The promulgators of the Bull thought that such magnanimity would be appreciated in Germany, and believed that the Bull would be obediently received.

So long had the papacy toyed with immorality, oppression and untruth that it was now unable to discern truth and righteousness. This was its last and bitterest punishment. All it could now see was what threatened its interests, what forwarded them. The former was wrong, the latter right. The hypocritical and sanctimonious unctuousness of the language of the Bull was the homage vice is compelled to pay to virtue, if vice is determined to prevail. But Rome only deceived herself, her own sycophants and a few good men who really believed her in spite of the evidence. Most of Germany treated the Bull with scorn and derision, smarting as they were from papal scandals. For the Pope to aver that he had been activated throughout the proceedings against Luther by purely religious motives and only in the interests of Germany, set a tone of utter insincerity to the manifesto. Not a word said about the glaring evils and the urgent necessity of reform. No mention of Luther's scriptural views, no refutation of the alleged heresies. To reassert the authority of the Church and the infallibility of the Pope as ultimate arbiter was to beg the question. No allowance was made for genuine scholarship, for conscientious difference of opinion. Never has leadership been more incompetent and irrelevant: never have consequences been so momentous. The naiveté of expecting a man of Luther's age, position and genius to recant without reasons, shows how far removed the Papal Curia was from its real office. It was ludicrous for the Pope to take on the role of the offended spiritual father, for he was a father without the respect of his family, without moral force, without paternal prestige. His absolutism, too, was anachronistic : Leo X was not a Gregory or an Innocent, and times had changed. The universal degeneration of the Church had fostered widespread revolt of her best sons. Further, the Renaissance with its new intellectualism and liberalism and its new tools of linguistic and historical criticism had brought a fresh spirit of enquiry into the West. Men would never again be handled in this way.

There was a further consideration. Luther had all along warned his critics that the Reformation was more than Luther. In condemning Luther the Pope was condemning men and movements that would brook no stay : the humanist movement and the new learning of the universities; a large class of the responsible nobility, even two of the princes, John Frederick and Barnim of Pomerania; most of the great cities and their local authorities; the middle class; nearly all the peasantry and artisans who saw in him (confusedly as time was to indicate) their only deliverer from Roman corruption, humbug and tyranny; to this long list should be added Luther's prince, the most powerful and respected of them all, and his government and associates. Only the Emperor appreciated this point; the religious establishment was stone blind. If the Church had been what the Bull depicted it, there might have been some point to the Bull. But the attempt to destroy Luther without an attempt to reform brooked disaster. A further gross blunder was to put this document in the hands of Aleander and Eck to promulgate, a mistake which Pallavicini himself regretted. Aleander was Italian, a Curialist, the champion of papal absolutism and traditional orthodoxy, a man Erasmus described as an evil man and a liar. He was hated in Germany and treated abominably wherever he went, even by landlords and innkeepers. Eck was known as a sworn enemy of Luther since his performance at Leipzig, and a notorious papalist. It would be difficult to instance in all the long human conflict for truth a declaration made and promulgated as idiotic as it was myopic.

The Weimarer editors point out (WA. 7. 152) that when the Bull *Exsurge, Domine* was finally published it virtually had no effect in Germany, the one place it was meant to bring to its knees. The secular princes left any initiative to be taken to the spiritual princes. Archbishops and bishops dilly-dallied in spiritual paralysis. The universities demurred on the technical grounds that the Bull was unsuitably drafted. The common people resisted it. Nobody was found to make the decisive step of implementing it. The Bull would have been an utter flop, had not Aleander, with Caracciolo, left Rome determined to put it into effect.

At once they proceeded to the court of the Empire in the Netherlands, and within three days had a bonfire going in Louvain, before the middle of October. On 12 November there was another at Cologne, another at Mainz on 29 November. At Mainz the public hangman refused to burn Luther's books at Aleander's command. The latter found a grave-digger willing to do so, but the students supplied him with Roman books, and gleefully watched him consigning these books to the flames instead of Luther's.

When Eck arrived in Leipzig to promulgate the Bull he found a Leipzig different from that he had left 'in triumph' a year earlier. He met hostile placards in the streets and was the butt of comic song and jest. The Wittenberg students came over and threatened mischief if he did not make himself scarce. Terrified, he fled to a monastery and then fled the town. The university refused to publish the Bull, and only did so the next year under the threat of Duke George. When it was eventually posted, it was pelted with filth and then torn up. The same happened in Torgau, Dobeln, Erfurt, and elsewhere: Wittenberg bluntly refused the papal mandate. Many bishops declined to act, or played delaying tactics: the Bishops of Naumburg, Freising, Augsburg, Passau, Bamberg, the Archbishop of Salzburg. Secular princes declined to publish it as destructive of public peace, and wanted action delayed until the Diet of Worms made its decisions. This was the line taken by Frederick when Aleander was pressing for action in Cologne. Eck had gone further even than Aleander. He added the names of a number of Luther's supporters who were to recant with Luther. A good deal of the opposition to Eck is to be attributed to the crass folly of handing the Bull to a chief disputant in the debate to execute. This incensed Germany. Luther's books were burned in Cologne, Louvain, Liège, Halberstadt, Ingolstadt and Mainz, but this did the perpetrators little good. It served to increase the opposition of the humanists and of the humanist knights, and drew not a little support for Luther.

Such activity certainly impressed the people: they thought that the Papal Curia meant business after all. These proceedings gave Erasmus much distress of mind. Luther wrote to Spalatin at the time that if they continued this line of action he would retaliate by burning publicly the whole canon law as hostile to the Gospel. When the bonfires drew nearer to Wittenberg, first at Merseburg with the threat of another at Leipzig, Luther took action. He notified Prince Frederick of his intention, and Melanchthon notified the university.

In the meantime there had been a considerable amount of robust sixteenth century polemics. Augustin von Alveld, a Franciscan of Leipzig, was urged by his bishop to write against Luther, though the Franciscans on the whole had shown not opposition to, but considerable interest in, Luther. Von Alveld was a man of learning but lacked all historical judgment and took the old scholastic line. He produced many pamphlets in particular, *On the Roman See,* but it was his work *On the Papal See* (short title) which provoked Luther to write his *On the Papacy at Rome,* June 1520 (WA. 6. 285ff.).

The importance of this work is that it presents in ever sharpening focus the real nature of Luther's protest as a protest against the papacy. It is also essentially part of Luther's defence. In it he reviews the attacks of all the papalists—Cajetan, Eck,

Emser, and the Cologne and Louvain theologians, and now Alveld. The question at issue, Luther argues, is whether the papal power, which all recognize, is of God or of man. Are all the Christians—Russians, Greeks, Bohemians—who did not buy their bishoprics from Rome, heretics, in spite of their same faith, their same baptism? Why do the Romanists not answer his arguments instead of reasserting indulgences and papal power?

Against Eck he wrote his *Eck's New Bulls and Lies* (WA. 6. 579–94) and also *Against the execrable Bull of Antichrist* (WA. 6. 597–612). He can scarcely bring himself to believe the authenticity of the documents, nor that Eck could be allowed, as a party in the dispute, to execute the Bull. He treats Eck with scorn and defends Huss against the decisions of the Council of Constance. The Pope he openly describes as Antichrist, and looks to the future with deep foreboding.

On 17 November 1520 Luther again appealed for a General Council and expressed his readiness to face examination. He begs the lay leadership of Christendom—Emperor, Electors, princes, the nobility and secular authority in general—to resist the folly and madness of the Pope, and to support his own appeal for a General Council. If they felt unable to offer resistance to the papacy, then at least they should not proceed against Luther until they had heard his case before impartial judges in the light of the appropriate evidence (WA. 7. 80–1). Luther then explained the history and significance of his case to the common people in non-technical language and in their mother tongue (WA. 7. 85–90), a document which went through eight editions in eight weeks. The former is rather an official document of the nature of a legal defence of Luther's position; the second is a perfect example of Luther's characteristic concern to inform the laity at every stage of the dispute, and to carry them along with him.

Luther was to strike a more dramatic blow. It had been his intention to burn the Bull from the pulpit of the parish church. This would have been a gesture worthy of an Old Testament prophet. As it turned out at 9 a.m. on 10 December 1520 he and the other professors with their students marched out to the carrion pit where Agricola had already kindled a fire. A fine old oak marks the spot to this day. Agricola consigned to the flames the volumes of the canon law, the *Summa Angelica,* together with some smaller volumes of Eck and Emser. The Canon Law embodied for Luther the confusion of Gospel with Law, of politics with religion, the making of the Kingdom of God into a temporal kingdom, the secularization of the spiritual, the setting up of the Pope in the room of God. The *Summa* embodied the intellectualization of these mistakes, the perversion of pastoral care into jurisprudence, the corruption of clergy into judges. As he watched them burn he very solemnly drew the Bull out of his cassock pocket. Unostentatiously he threw it on the top of the pyre mumbling a prayer to the effect that as the Bull had betrayed Christ, may it eternally perish. He watched it burn, turned on his heel, and quietly returned to his study to pursue his day's work.

A thrill went through Europe when it learned that an obscure monk, a man with no more weight behind him than his faith in God, had burned a papal Bull. It was the fiery signal of emancipation. The individual had asserted his true value. If the Reformation can be dated, that date must be 10 December 1520. If eras can be dated as Gordon Rupp expressed it, our modern era began at nine o'clock that morning.

It was a dramatic end to a year of prodigious writing—*On Good Works, Treatise on the New Testament, An Appeal to the Nobility, The Babylonian Captivity, The Freedom of a Christian Man,* to name some of the most influential. If not all had seen the significance of his writings none could evermore doubt his mind and purpose.

Rome had now no course open to it except to excommunicate the rebel and execute the threats of *Exsurge, Domine.* The 'holy curse' was drawn up and signed in Rome on 3 January 1521 and sent to Cardinal Aleander to promulgate. The document put

Luther and others (von Hutten, Pirkheimer, Spengler) under the ban, and even went so far as to condemn Frederick. Aleander was apprehensive when he read the document and returned it to Rome for modification, fearing that as it then stood, greater harm could ensue to the Church than to Luther and his supporters. It was modified and the name of Luther only appeared in the final draft, the Bull *Decet Romanum Pontificem.** It was finally published at Worms on 6 May 1521, some three weeks after he had been heard at the Diet.

The Bull adds nothing more to the earlier one, which it actually incorporated verbatim in its text. By canon law a heretic had the right to repent after the promulgation of the bull condemning him, and this explains why it is the second bull which excommunicates Luther since he had not repented after the first.

The Bull gives a long preamble about the Pope's responsibilities in issuing Bulls to destroy heresy and schism in the Church and to further its unity. He argues that since the publication of the first Bull many of Luther's followers have deserted him and returned to the Catholic Faith; and many of Luther's books publicly burnt. Luther himself, however, has gone from bad to worse and led astray many followers. The Pope thereby anathematizes Martin and his followers and decrees that they have incurred all the punishments proscribed. They shall all bear the name 'Lutheran'. The censure is decreed on all who help, counsel or favour Luther and his followers, no matter how high or noble the family. They and all their descendants are to be deprived of all dignities, honours and goods. Their possessions are to be confiscated. They themselves are to be charged with high treason.

All places where these heretics have lived or to which they have resorted are to be set under an interdict. All such men are to be denounced publicly by name, anathematized, deprived of all possessions, and disallowed from holding any.

* Turin Bullarium. Tome V. 761–4 (1860), or any standard Bullarium.

The Pope commands as a positive step more impassioned preaching against the heresies of Martin.

The upshot of this second Bull was that Luther was now excommunicated, and that it was the responsibility of the secular arm to execute the mandate. The two bulls obviously belong together, the second being in effect the official confirmation of the first, the second (*Decet Romanum* 3 January 1521) brings us a little ahead of our story, and we must return to the original Bull (*Exsurge, Domine* June 1520) which we last saw burning on the pyre outside the gates of Wittenberg on the cold dark morning of 10 December 1520.

There was more to the burning of the Papal Bull and canon law than the brandishing of the torch of revolution. It was imperative at this hour that Luther should now stand on the world stage, and stand there with the support of his university. The solemn burning of the bull and canon law by the professors, in company with university officers and students, convinced the Papal Curia that they had on their hands not a man but a movement, and demonstrated to the world that the University of Wittenberg supported its famous professor, heart and mind.

Luther was not satisfied with expressing his contempt for the Bull, with defending his own teaching, and with exposing the anti-biblical nature of the Romanist doctrines, but he answered back in kind. Rome had short-sightedly proclaimed him a heretic: he answered back that Rome was both heretical and schismatic. Rome had excommunicated him on her own authority: he excommunicated Rome quoting Jesus Christ as his authority and judge. Rome had burnt his books, he burnt hers. This was a public, collective, responsible, flagrant secession from Rome, which spoke more effectively than many theological volumes.

Luther was fully aware of what he had done. He had entered the arena to fight the Pope and the papacy, and all he had on his side were his own faith and his learning. The authority of evidential truth here challenged all authority. The fiery

G

signal of emancipation beamed throughout Europe, and has not yet been extinguished. The individual soul had discovered its true value, and mankind has never gone back on this, save in its darkest moments, yet always to recover. Gravely and earnestly Luther addressed his students the next morning as they were sitting at their desks waiting for him to continue his lectures on the Psalms. He told them the grounds of his action, and what amounted to his break with the papacy.

There were more than students expecting an explanation of this unique and consequential deed, and to the world at large Luther gave a justification of his actions in a German tract* which was also an explanation of the issues at stake. The situation Luther precipitated was desperately delicate and dangerous, for Pope, prelates, princes and people were dumbfounded at such an act, never heard of in the history of man. Doggedly Luther gave a terse analysis of the vital differences between the two conceptions of religion, and indicated the foundations of true evangelical Christianity. Canon law and papal authority are set on one side, evangelical theology and biblical authority beside it. All men may judge for themselves the truth of the two positions.

The importance of the document in a book on the trial of Luther is that it sets out in a contemporary form his debate with the papacy at an earlier stage than it emerged at his final trial proper at Worms. At Worms insufficient time was given to the debate, for the whole purpose at that time was to prevent Luther speaking and to wrest from him a recantation. This document really belongs to the evidence on which he was judged at Worms.

In the pamphlet he gave his reasons for burning the Bull and the papalist books. On the precedent of the Acts of the Apostles he gave his authority. As a doctor of theology, under oath, it was his duty to destroy all false, seductive and unchristian

* *Why the books of the Pope and his disciples were burnt by Dr. Martin Luther.* WA. 7. 161ff.

doctrine. He was not prepared under God's Spirit idly to stand by and do nothing. He had demonstrated the theological and spiritual errors of the Pope and the papalists, and all they had done was to condemn and burn the doctrine of Christ and to uphold and pursue their own anti-Christian, demoniacal teaching. He added that the burning of his books at the Universities of Cologne and Louvain had only been effected by heavy bribery of the civil power. This conduct could lead to the shipwreck of truth in the eyes of the uneducated populace, he had retaliated on the papal books to preserve truth. He quoted freely from the canon law, saying, 'The sum and substance of the canon law is this: the Pope is God upon earth, superior to every other being, celestial or terrestrial, spiritual or secular. All things appertain to the Pope, and nobody dare ask him, "What doest thou?" Luther described such pretensions as proving that 'the abomination of desolation was standing in the holy place' (Dan. 11.31). No one was to allow himself to be brow-beaten in face of the prestige of the papal books but to examine them for himself and note the false teaching of the canon law.

Luther had been making a deep study of the canon law during the past two years and he drew up a list of papal claims which he dubbed as erroneous. Among these were the claim to be independent of God's command; the claim of the spiritual power to be superior to the temporal; the claim of the Church to be above Councils and in control of all law; the claim of the Roman See to be beyond all legal control even for evil Popes to be above any condemnation or judgment; the claim to fealty of all bishops; the claim of all supremacy based on the Petrine succession; the claim to make laws for the Christian Church. There was also the claim to prescribe all laws for the life of the Church, feast days and fast days, priestly celibacy and the like. He refers further to the political claims of Rome based on the supposed Donation of Constantine* and the false

*This document purported to be the testament of Emperor Constantine (306–37). It conveyed to the Pope title to the city of Rome, certain lands

decretals of Isidore,* and how these had developed into the assumption by the Church of the legacy of power left by the Roman Empire. Here the Pope claimed the right to dethrone kings, to release from oaths as well as political and legal obligations, to remit religious vows. Luther's concern in all this was that canon law had been elevated to equality with the Gospels, even subsumed its authority, and that the Pope claimed to be the sole interpreter of Scripture.

The importance of all this, though but a pamphlet, is, as has been argued, that it reveals Luther's defence of his case before his trial. The papal claim to be above all human judgment, with the derivative right to judge all men, was the expression of this corpus of canon law, the fecund source of the world's misfortunes. Spiritual power, Luther argued, springs from humility and is not buttressed by exterior authority. The true mark of the Church was that of a servant not a mistress. The proposition that the authority of Scripture derived from the Pope makes not only man subject to him but God. Canon law has made a god of the Pope. It is in this sense, and in this biblical sense only, in the direct line of the teaching of Christ, of John and of Paul, that Luther calls the Pope the Antichrist.

in Italy, and 'the islands of the sea'. Medieval pontiffs used the document to support their claims to temporal power. In 1440 Laurentius Valla, an Italian humanist, exposed the Donation as an eighth-century forgery. Ulrich von Hutten's 1517 republication of Valla's exposé came to Luther's attention just before he wrote the present treatise. Luther published an annotated translation of the Donation in 1537. WA 50. 60–89.

*A collection of documents attributed to Isidore of Seville (d. 636) but really compiled in France about 850. It contains: (1) letters of ante-Nicene Popes (all forgeries); (2) a collection of canons, mainly genuine; (3) a collection of letters of Popes, many of which are spurious. The compiler collected these false and half-true documents with remarkable skill, designed essentially to maintain the supremacy of the papacy. When first used they were known to be forgeries but by the Middle Ages antiquity had lent them such authority that Thomas More and John Fisher used them in their anti-Protestant writings. Their genuineness was disproved by 1558 and the decretals are now universally rejected.

It is that the Pope has usurped the place of Christ: the greatest evil always arises in the holiest place—Lucifer was revealed in heaven, Christ crucified in Jerusalem, Rome has produced the Antichrist. The Pope, Luther argues, has never defeated anybody with Scripture or reasonable argument. His only attack is the ban, violence, or trickery. He argued that he was accepting full responsibility for what he was saying.

The document was avidly read. Ten editions appeared within a month, and two Latin editions in Wittenberg and Worms. It is interesting to note that Cuthbert Tunstall, the ambassador at the court of Charles V, and later to become Bishop of Durham, sent a copy of it to Cardinal Wolsey with the covering note that it was known all over Germany.

This was tantamount to a declaration of war, and we must see in the burning of the Bull, followed by Luther's justification of his act, the transition of the evangelical cause from the explanatory to the offensive. Luther was now a master of Scripture and had been teaching biblical theology years before Tetzel obtruded. The indulgence scandal, far from producing the Reformation, found the Reformation already in existence: it was simply the spark that fired the train. But, from the assertion of truth Luther had now advanced into the controversial area of the detection of error. He had made an advance which had been denied Christendom for over a thousand years. Whereas Athanasius in the fourth century had established the truth of Christ in the area of mind and doctrine, and had established this in the teeth of the opposition of paganism and Gnosticism, Luther now advanced from the area of knowing into the realm of being, from the knowing the truth to the doing the truth. His evangelical theology drove him to condemn the worldliness and secularity of the doctrinal system of the Church of Rome in order to establish biblical doctrine. All this had been a long and gradual process over about twelve years. The papalist fictions had been exposed one by one under the searchlight of Scripture and reason. Even his opponents subserved his purpose, for none sought to listen to him and then answer him, but only to silence him and to reassert more violently than before the very doctrines he had found erroneous and unjustifiable. Luther had reached the height of his antipapalism now and realized there could be only one outcome, an open and public challenge of papal authority with a declaration of his biblical theology.

Luther gave an energetic defence of his position in answering the case for the prosecution presented by the Pope and his advisers in the Bull *Exsurge, Domine,* with particular reference to the forty-one errors selected by the prosecution from Luther's writings. He gave his defence in four works, two in German and two in Latin: *Against the execrable Bull of the Antichrist* November 1520 (WA. 6. 595ff), *Against the Bull of Antichrist* November 1520 (WA. 6. 613ff), *A Defence of all the Articles of Martin Luther condemned in the most recent Bull of Leo X* December 1520 (WA. 7. 91ff), and *Defence and Explanation of all the Articles of Dr Martin Luther so wrongly condemned in the Romish Bull* March 1521 (WA. 7. 299ff).

The arguments of these writings are essential to a proper understanding of Luther's position, and though not presented in court are basic to his case against the papal prosecution. The writings are of book-length and are, therefore, too long to be incorporated verbatim in the present book, but an epitome of the argument taken from the last work follows. The last work is selected because Luther himself considered it 'smoother and simpler' than the others. The first and third are in Latin and directed to the clergy and scholars. The second and fourth are in German and of wider appeal. Though Luther preferred the fourth vernacular version the writer considers this version to be less trenchant and less effective theologically than the December Latin draft.

Epitome of Luther's Defence and Explanation

Before he turns to give a specific answer to each of the forty-one articles, he offers a general explanatory statement of his position by way of introduction.

His first word is one of thanks to God who has enlightened so many people in his day, not least the laity. People all the world over can now distinguish between the true and counterfeit church: to see through all the formalities and externalities that had hitherto passed for the Church as well as through the leadership such a church got for itself. Men could now see beyond all this falsity to the true New Testament doctrine of the Church as the called people of God. It was the deplorable and secularized clergy that in its utterly blind confusion had produced a Bull that had made it the laughing stock of Christendom.

Luther argues that the Reformation is a movement of God and prays that men will properly respond to this divine activity. He intends to defend every single one of his articles from Scripture and to expose the false Church for what it is, in the hopes that it will reform.

First, he defends himself. He is not caustic and impatient as alleged. In doctrine he is sober and sound, only in the controversies about foolish matters on the periphery such as indulgences is he impatient, controversies he never began and which are not worthy of serious argument.

He was accused of vaingloriously setting up himself as the teacher of the world. But anybody who knew him, knew him as shy and retiring. Be that as it may, suppose God was addressing the Church through him? Ought his words not to be considered on their merit? They argued his voice was a lone voice in Christendom. Had not God always spoken with a lone voice? Moses, Elijah, Elisha, Isaiah, Jeremiah, Ezekiel were all lone men. Had not God always raised up lowly persons for his messengers, never the lofty, never the high priests of this world? The called of God had always found themselves against kings, priests and scholars. Today it was the same. Everything not agreeable to the Pope, the bishops and the scholars was assumed wrong. Luther gave further examples from the New Testament and from Church history. Luther did not claim to be a prophet, but he had the Word of God on his side and his enemies had not.

His enemies accuse him of novelty of doctrine. So were the prophets accused, and the apostles, and Christ himself. But Luther claimed he said nothing new, but that Christianity had perished among those very men who ought to have preserved it, the bishops and scholars. But he had no doubt that the laity and common folk had kept the essentials in their hearts, as Jeremiah experienced (Jeremiah 5.4f): likewise the common people understood Luther better than the leaders.

In argument or enquiry it is not how long a matter has been believed but whether it is true. It is not Catholic tradition that convinces but the truth of Scripture. The demand is to examine the reason and ground of all we believe and practise. It is wrong to accuse a person of rejecting the doctors of the Church. Men are errant. Luther wants every opinion and tradition to be critically examined before the bar of Scripture: this the great Church Fathers did, e.g. Augustine. The lie has always the greater following, the truth the smaller. Truth has always caused a disturbance, but an uproar does not prove false the teaching that caused it. Luther here cites Paul's experiences in Acts, as well as those of Ezekiel and Jeremiah. If Luther is but one poor body against the might of the Church, he at least commends his cause to God and His Truth, which the Pope is now condemning.

Luther then turns to the discussion of the 41 articles which the Pope had extracted from his writings (p. 84–8) and which he had declared heretical. Luther defends or explains the points seriatim. The text (100 pages) is of some importance to Luther's case but only a brief survey of the contents may be made here.

The first article is a repudiation of the prevalent teaching that the efficacy of the sacraments remains, provided a recipient 'raises no barriers'. Luther argues that the Catholic view is erroneous and not in accordance with Scripture, Catholic and

Patristic tradition, and common sense. To receive the sacraments was an exercise of prayer for grace, and this demanded faith and belief in forgiveness: it was absurd to argue the sacraments were efficacious as long as no 'obstacle' was raised by the recipient.

On Article 2, that sin remains after baptism, Luther adduced the teaching of Christ, the work of Paul and John and a good deal of other scriptural evidence, as well as the plain evidence of one's own experience. Luther makes a plea to be done with the scholastic jugglery with words and to take the biblical words in their plain meaning. A man must speak of words such as faith, love, hope, grace, sin, law as clearly as he differentiates between a tree and a stone, a horse and a cow. Sin just does not disappear after baptism. A man's life is an unending conflict with sin. The conflict is important. True life is not godliness but the process of becoming godly, not health but getting better, not being but becoming, not rest but work: it is less what we are now, but what we are growing into; this life is not the goal, rather it furnishes the right road; we do not gleam and sparkle now, but we are being polished up. Article 3 argues the same point.

On Article 4 Luther justifies his view that it is an inadequate love of God that brings fear of death and that he knows nothing about purgatory. He handles the related ideas of penance and indulgences in Article 5 arguing that they are taught neither by Scripture nor Catholic tradition but are innovations which may properly be described as 'lies and deceit'. In Article 6 he defends his teaching on contrition. The Roman view of dwelling on sin and inducing a feeling of contrition led to all the abuses of 'Judas contrition', 'gallows contrition' and other deathbed scrambles. The true Catholic doctrine of contrition arises from the penitent heart. It is not a dwelling on sin, otherwise Judas would have known contrition. Such forced and imagined contrition is feigned. True contrition is a gift from God, the work of the Holy Spirit, the grace of which he spoke in Article 1. The point is pursued in the next article, No. 7, where he demonstrates that when God's contrition sets in the whole man undergoes a transformation. This is a disturbing and destructive experience but it means the outpouring of God's grace and strength in the secular experiences of life. On the papal claim to 'Whatever you loose on earth shall be loosed in heaven', he writes, 'In these words Christ does not confer authority, but rather he moves every Christian heart to faith so that when a man is absolved by the priest he may be assured that he is absolved by God. The power of the keys accomplishes no more than you believe and not as much as the Pope and his followers choose! In fact in confession a man must rely on God's grace and not his own contrition, confession and satisfaction (Article 8); on God's mercy never his own works or the power of the Pope (Article 9).'

The Pope simply condemns the Christian doctrine of the forgiveness of sins in Article 10. Not even Christ ascribes the forgiveness of sins to his own absolution, to his keys, to his power, but to faith. How can the Pope act to the contrary? Every man knows that the priest's absolution is a verdict of God not of himself. The priest offers what Christ offered : God's forgiveness to a sinner. Further (Article 11 and 12), if a man did not put his trust in God alone, he would be bound to believe that he could attain forgiveness and grace by his own contrition and merit. Can any man confront God with his own worthiness? The Bull is erroneous: it is tantamount to a denial of grace, a loss of the Gospel. Any Christian lay man may offer all that popes and priests offer (Article 13). No man may build on his own contrition (Article 14), nor have confidence in his own confession (Article 15): it is all a matter of faith not works, and works issue from faith, not vice versa.

In Article 16 the Pope condemns Luther's teaching that the laity should receive the communion in both kinds (i.e. both bread and wine). Luther replies on the grounds that Christ so instituted the Last Supper and from Paul on, such has been the practice of the Church. Luther here quotes the practice of the Orthodox Church in support of his view as well as of conciliar pronouncement. Luther is perfectly aware that the full sacrament may be received in faith without bread or wine. He is not inciting revolt as alleged but seeking to restore biblical and Catholic practice in the Church. Christendom has deserved this papal tyranny: Luther submits to it for it cannot hurt the soul to submit, but that does not require him to be silent or to call a tyrant 'Holy Father'. Luther is teaching plain and verifiable tradition.

The Pope turns to the matter of indulgences in Articles 17–22. It is sheer invention, Luther argues, to describe indulgences as drawing spiritual credit from the Treasury of Merits, a limitless storehouse allegedly accumulated by Christ and the saints. The Pope can grant an indulgence only to a disciplinary penalty he has imposed. The Pope assumes the divine role of remitting sin, and charges fees for it. The whole affair (Article 18) is a 'pious fraud' and a diabolical scheme whereby the Pope 'peddles sin' to raise money. The Pope with all his lackeys would have been beggars long ago if they had not had Christ to sell and exploit.

Article 23 criticizes Luther's teaching on excommunication. He argues that as the Pope had usurped the power of God in claiming to save souls by indulgences, by the same usurpation he claims to damn souls by means of the power of excommunication. A man of faith neither death, nor hell, nor even sin can harm. Excommunication relates only to things external, i.e. exclusion from the fellowship of the Church and from the sacraments. Further, the true teaching of canon law considers the ban a remedial medicine not a destructive agency. For this reason (Article 24) a man should love the ban if it were properly administered.

In Article 25 the Pope singles out Luther's teaching that the Pope is not the Vicar of Christ, by Christ's appointment supreme over all churches of the world. Luther defends his view that when the papacy usurps this role for itself it replaces Christ by the Pope and abolishes the Gospel. He begins by showing that there is nothing in the Bible on the subject of the papacy. To defend the view of the primacy of the Pope is to violate the Bible and to revile the countless Christians (in Africa, Greece, the Near East and elsewhere) who do not recognize the Pope. The Pope argues that to be a Christian one must owe allegiance to Rome, but Christ and Paul bound it only to faith and God's Word (about which the Pope and his henchmen know nothing).

Luther then examines the key passage, 'Thou art Peter and upon this rock I will build my church; and the gates of hell shall not prevail against it. And I will give unto thee the keys of the kingdom of heaven: and whatsoever thou shalt bind on earth shall be bound in heaven : and whatsoever thou shalt loose on earth shall be loosed in heaven' (Matt. 16. 18–20). He argues that the papalists interpret the rock to mean Peter, and assume that it is the papal power on which Christ builds his church, and that therefore all churches ought to be subject to the Pope's power. According to these interpreters the church built on the rock means the church subject to the Pope.

But, Luther argues, if to build the church upon a rock means to submit it to the Pope, then a church could be founded and could exist without faith and without the Gospel. The power and authority of the Pope is one thing: faith, sacraments and gospel another. That the gates of hell shall not prevail against the church cannot mean against papal power for this building has patently collapsed and the gates of hell have manifestly prevailed against it. All Christendom has fallen away from the Pope; in fact, it was never built on this 'rock': Greeks, Africans, Bohemians and Orientals are not built on this 'rock'.

But to turn to the plain meaning of the words. The rock on which the Church is founded is Christ, and the building founded on that rock is the believing church. Against Christ and men of faith the gates of hell can never prevail. It is illegitimate exegesis to interpret this text as referring to papal power and rule, a point that Huss made a century earlier. The text is about faith not papal power. It is just not good enough to quote some few Fathers in support of the papalistic exegesis against the plain meaning of Christ's words.

The other proof text, 'Lovest thou me? Feed my sheep' (John 21. 15–19) cannot be used to prove that the Pope is over all Christians. The real meaning undermines the papacy: on this occasion Christ is demanding love of Peter and his responsibility to tend, teach and care for the faithful at the cost of his life. On these criteria the papacy is as much use to Christendom as a fifth wheel to a wagon.

Further, New Testament evidence clearly shows that Peter was an apostle and a servant of the other apostles. Peter created no apostles, but was one of the Twelve. All bishops are equal, not under one sovereign power, but in the unity of faith.

Article 26 continues the Matthaean text in the matter of 'Whatever you loose on earth shall be loosed in heaven'. To interpret this text to give power to the Pope over purgatory, as well as heaven and hell, is for the Pope to arrogate to himself the role of God. Neither is it right to apply them to the remission of penalties. These words of Christ did not give a power to Peter, who is only a servant of the Gospel. They are the promise of absolution and forgiveness here on earth given by Christ, the common property of all.

Article 27 refers to Luther's denial of the Pope's or the Church's right to establish articles of faith and commandments regarding morals and good works. To do so is for the Pope to arrogate to himself the office of Christ and the Holy Spirit, a claim expressly against the teaching of Christ and of the Apostles. The Pope in referring to Article 28 denies the right of anybody to disagree with him, but in matters not necessary to salvation disagreement is neither sin nor heresy. Luther also argues that many recent Councils have debated useless and frivolous matters to the great confusion of the Church.

In Article 29 on Councils Luther says his view is not to teach that anybody may question Councils arbitrarily but that the Church is to measure their proceedings by appeal to Scripture which is superior to all Councils. This is sound canon law, not heresy.

In Article 30 the Pope instances Luther's approval of the doctrines of John Huss, a man condemned by lawful Council. Luther replies that he has gone much further than Huss, and yet has not gone far enough. Luther repeats that the papacy is a human invention, and that unity depends on sound doctrine not on the sovereignty of the Pope. Luther claims also to have gone beyond Wycliffe's criticism of the decretals.

In support of Article 31, that a good man still sins in all his good works, Luther adduces the evidence of the saints and Church Fathers as well as the Bible and common experience. The papalists evade the plain teaching of Scripture on sin by fabricating sophistries and words in its place. All men are sinners: no man living is justified in God's sight. The papalists resist this doctrine because they trust not in God and his mercy but in their own works-righteousness. Luther would rather stand condemned with Isaiah, David, Solomon, Paul, Augustine and Gregory than praised with the Pope and the papalists. The same point is made in Articles 32 and 35.

Article 33 concerns Luther's words that to burn heretics is contrary to the will of God. In support, if support were necessary, Luther argues that the Church has never burned its heretics until recent times, and certainly the Bible does not teach the doctrine. By canon law clergy are forbidden to bear arms, yet no one spills more blood than the Holy Father with his guns and swords. 'If the Pope were to defend himself in books, he could not last an instant,' Luther says. 'Why do they not answer my writings?'

The Pope singles out Luther's objection to the crusades in Article 34. Luther argues that Christendom is blind to the wrongness of war with the Turk and to the Pope's semi-militaristic role which causes much misery and destruction, though it talks of crusading indulgences and promises of heaven. Luther argues that God does not want crusades, indulgences and wars: He wants Christendom to mend its ways. Luther believes that everything is going wrong in Europe because God is warring against its wickedness, and that the meaning of God's 'hostility' is to bring Christendom to repentance.

Article 36 refers to Luther's teaching on the unfree will. This matter is central to Luther's thinking and developed into the debate between Erasmus and Luther in 1525. Luther argues that without God's grace the will is free only to sin. He dislikes the non-scriptural phrase 'free will', which he interprets as 'self will'. If one uses the phrase 'free will', that can only properly be applied to the man newly created in Christ by grace. A man in sin is his own prisoner: a man in grace may become free by the operation of God's grace.

Articles 37–40 refer to Luther's agnostic views on purgatory. He replies by criticizing the spurious proofs that Rome offered, and argues that men who reject this idea cannot therefore be called heretics on that account. The entire Orthodox Church of the East repudiates the doctrine of purgatory, yet it is still a true part of the Church Catholic. Luther knows that Peter and James were saints, but that does not mean that he is compelled to believe that Peter lies buried at Rome and James at Compostella. Luther may not think that all the people the Pope canonizes are saints, but that does not make Luther a heretic. (The saints in question would not take offence at Luther!) Luther refers to the abuses and scandals arising from the doctrine, 'the papacy and the whole hierarchy are all built upon purgatory, and derive all their wealth and honour from it. The majority of the priests would starve to death if there were no purgatory.' Luther's view is that there are neither scriptural nor rational arguments in support of purgatory, simply vested interest: the whole matter is open to debate, and ought to remain so.

The final article selected as heretical (41) refers to Luther's view that the mendicant orders should be dissolved. A priest's responsibility is to preach and minister, not to go around begging. The Jews forbade all begging, and so ought the Christians who elevate begging to a special Christian estate.

Finally Luther deplores the fact that in this affair he has John Eck for his opponent, for obviously the Bull is his handiwork. He regrets that he has to have liars and villains for opponents instead of godly and honourable men who would discuss the issues truly. A historian can only echo the same regret. Had Luther had the worthy and competent Catholics with whom to discuss the crisis, of whom there were very many, the whole debate would have gone otherwise and Christendom would never have been divided.

The reader should not underestimate the importance of this document in Luther's debate with Rome. Luther entitled the book *Defence and Explanation,* and that is an exact description of its contents.

It should be appreciated before we look at the Diet of Worms, that the movement of which Luther was the protagonist was in all essentials a religious doctrinal movement, with important elements of a literary as well as a socio-politico-nationalist movement, with which latter elements Luther had little sympathy or interest. To Luther the centre and circumference were evangelical truth, yet the other movements excited public interest, and sometimes extended the influence of the Reformation, even if they confounded the true issues. Nevertheless, these elements were there—many of the humanists and educated laity were interested in Luther for his rebellion against scholasticism, many nationalists for his magnificent resistance to tyranny and extortion. In a real sense Luther's character embraced all these three elements, nevertheless the religious and theological dominated the humanist and nationalist, as it did for the classical Reformation proper.

Humanly speaking Luther's cause looked hopeless. True, there were encouraging signs. The movement was already astir in other countries, such as Denmark and Switzerland. Luther's pupils were beginning to occupy the chairs and the pulpits, at home and abroad. Frederick showed himself prepared to shelter Luther and his cause. The University of Wittenberg was solidly behind him. Popular sentiment was strongly in his favour. But the question may appropriately be put, what chance did this band of reformers have against the organized might of Rome, with its centuries long tradition, its universally recognized authority, its devoted orders of monks, its subservient and interested allies in every town and village? There was no historical precedent where Rome had not routed and put to silence every reformer. There was increasing evidence that the Catholic Emperor would oppose the Reformation and support the Pope. Pope and Emperor identified themselves with authority against enquiry, precedent against reason, tradition against learning. The Emperor had already shown himself willing to burn Luther's books at the command of the Pope, and political realism would compel him to side with the Pope against Francis I. Against Pope and Emperor, the spiritual and the temporal lords, how slender were the unorganized forces of one territorial prince, one university, some knights, some merchants, some doctors and men of letters, some peasants and mechanics, and one university professor of theology to inspire and lead them.

The improbability of success did not deter Luther. On the contrary, it was part of his undying hope. The weakness of the human arm produced a more certain reliance on the divine arm. He was never even certain of his physical safety from the wiles of Rome, yet this made him trust the cause and not himself. 'My life will be the bane of the papacy, my death its ruin.'

H

4 The Trial at Worms

15 January–18 April 1521

The trial at Worms fell into five clearly defined stages. The first was the speech for the prosecution given by Cardinal Aleander on 18 January 1521 wherein he adumbrated the main charges (already given in the Bull *Exsurge, Domine*) and counselled the Diet that its task was not to examine and try Luther but, as the secular authority, solely to put into effect what the spiritual arm had already decreed in the Bull.

The second stage was the long discussions by the princes and estates with the Emperor which ensued, not only on the Luther affair, but on the malaise that had stricken the entire Holy Roman Empire in all its political, economic, social, military and even civic ramifications. The outcome of this debate was, among other decisions, that Luther be summoned to the Diet under the safe conduct of the Emperor.

The third stage was the first appearance of Luther on 18 April when he was asked if he was the author of the books exhibited in court and whether he would recant. On this brief appearance, awed by the situation, bewildered by such irregular procedure and perceiving the trap of such a peremptory and leading question which had already prejudged the issue, Luther asked for time to consider his reply.

The fourth stage was his second appearance on the next day 19 April when, contrary to the plans of the prosecution, Luther contrived a lengthy *excursus* in his defence which was also an explanation of his position. It is the proceedings of this day, the accusations of the prosecution and Luther's answers, which constitute the trial proper. These will be incorporated *verbatim* in our account of the trial.

The fifth stage is less generally appreciated and yet it was at this stage that the outcome of the trial hung in the balance. This stage is that of the long series of meetings arranged by some of the best Catholic minds at Worms to seek to find a *modus vivendi* at the eleventh hour. From 19–26 April these men tirelessly sought with Luther and his advisers some way in which the debate could be kept open, settled on an ecumenical basis, and the impending schism averted. They had Charles' approval of the proceedings if not his support. It is a bitter truth that both sides had to admit defeat.

Aleander's speech for the Prosecution 18 January 1521

The speech of Cardinal Aleander needs putting into its historical setting. Charles had created a new situation of expectancy in Germany when he travelled to Aachen to be crowned in the Cathedral on 23 October 1520. For some months there had been correspondence with the Electors as to the time and place of the too-long-deferred Diet, and now that he was actually on German soil, and about to begin the Diet there was a feeling in Germany of impending decisions. There was, too, in Germany, a universal conviction that Rome had mismanaged the whole Luther affair from beginning to end, and this feeling had captured not only the imperial estates but the peasants, too.

Two major issues dominated the German mind at this hour: imperial reform and church reform. In the matter of imperial reform the Estates sought for a weakening and restriction of imperial power and authority with the corresponding increase of their own. They wanted a Council of Regency, *Reichsregiment*, to act in the Emperor's absence, a council which would also restrict his powers in his presence. They sought also a new jurisdiction of the imperial chamber called the *Reichskammer*, the Imperial Court of Justice. In the matter of church reform it was the Luther affair which dominated minds more than the political questions just mentioned. People and princes wanted a renewed assertion of the sovereignty of the prince over his territorial Church; a limitation of clerical privileges particularly in the areas of law and of taxation; the rejection of any interference of the Pope in German church affairs. All this was desired even by those princes unsympathetic to Luther. Those who were sympathetic desired further an evangelical reformation of religion.

In Aachen the plague broke out, so the Emperor promptly removed to Cologne with his royal suite, accompanied by Aleander. Here on 31 October he met the Elector Frederick who had been held up with gout and unable to reach Aachen for the coronation. Frederick gave Charles a letter from Luther which appealed to the Emperor for justice and a fair hearing. To this Charles promised that Luther would be judged according to law.

Immediately after, on 4 November, Aleander sought an audience with Frederick. Aleander handed the prince a letter which certified that he was commissioned by the Pope and demanded two things: first, that the heretic's books be burned, and secondly that Frederick should punish Luther himself or hand him over to Aleander bound in execution of the Bull. It will be recalled that Aleander had already secured imperial authority to hold several public burnings of Luther's books in the Low Countries a few weeks earlier.

Frederick sought the advice of Erasmus, at that moment in Cologne. When asked what in his judgment Luther had done wrong, Erasmus wittily replied, 'He hit the Pope on the crown and the monks in their bellies!' Erasmus then drew up a document listing some of the issues which Luther had raised and which ought to be brought before a council of learned and impartial men. Strengthened by this intelligent reply, Frederick adroitly refused to grant the nuncios their demands. He professed utter innocence of any charge of complicity, explained the fact of not executing the Bull on the grounds that the case was before the Archbishop of Trier at that moment and still *sub judice,* and requested an impartial hearing of the kind Erasmus had recommended. Aleander argued that the Pope himself had taken over the case out of the hands of the Archbishop of Trier, and that it was the Pope's judgment expressed in the Bull which was decisive and could not be evaded. Frederick admitted the force of this in canon law, but pointed out that in Imperial Law a German subject had the right of appeal. It was a great tragedy for Christendom that the papacy rejected the counsel of Erasmus. Erasmus was deeply disquieted and saw with foreboding the impending disruption of Christendom.

Erasmus was not without support. He had the ear of the learned world and the respect of many princes. Glapion, father confessor to Charles, was favourably disposed to the Erasmian plan, as was John Faber, the Dominican, but William of Croy, the Lord of Chièvres and Gattinara, his old Grand Chancellor, the real advisory powers behind the imperial throne, were inflexibly opposed to the idea. The latter represented the mind of Rome, and looked with extreme distaste on any idea of Luther's theology being discussed in public or examined by any court other than their own. To them Luther's teachings were *res adjudicatae.* There was no reason to allow Luther the opportunity to maintain or defend them. They were already condemned. All that was now required was for the secular arm to punish the man the spiritual arm had already condemned. Aleander was inflexible and unrelenting. He was so successful that on 17 December (RA. II. 468) the Emperor revoked the invitation to the Elector to present Luther at Worms which he had made on 28 November (RA. II. 466). The Emperor expressed the view that Luther could be brought to the Worms area only after he had recanted. Otherwise, it would confuse the issue at home and spread misunderstanding abroad. Were Luther to recant, he would in that event be brought, say, to Frankfurt and there held until authoritative decisions about his future had been made. Were he to refuse to recant, he was to remain at Wittenberg until the Emperor and Frederick had decided what to do with him. The reason for this change of policy was the recent rapprochement of Pope and Emperor against Francis I.

Two significant matters may be discerned behind this correspondence. The first is Aleander's consuming concern that Luther be prevented from speaking, writing or publishing one more word, and that all that he had written be destroyed. There was dread lest Luther capture the ear and eye of the world. The second, again attributable to Aleander, was to make Luther out as the subverter of all political, social and spiritual authority. Aleander never changed his mind on these issues, and patently wrong though they were, persuaded Charles of their truth. Luther, and here he had much support from the learned world, placed his confidence in the free and open discussion of his case before competent and impartial judges, a course the papalists had every reason to fear. Aleander, and with him the papalists generally, misinterpreted Luther's dragging the Pope to the bar of common justice, sound learning and Christian principles as a frontal attack on all authority, spiritual in the first instance but eventually secular, too. This second charge was reiterated *ad nauseam,* but falsity is no less false for being oft repeated and widely held.

In reply to the Emperor's letter of 17 December Frederick wrote (28 December) that the letter had reached him when he was already half-way to Worms. He begged the Emperor to excuse him for not going back home to fetch Luther, although it is clear that Frederick did not want to involve himself to the extent of including Luther in his entourage.

The delivery of this letter at Worms brought about a new situation and a change of plan. It was realized that Frederick was near Worms and would arrive without Luther after all. About the end of December or the beginning of January the Emperor had decided on a delegation to handle the Luther affair, but with the certain non-arrival of Luther the plan fell through. The delegation had been planned to consist of the Bishop of Triest and Judocus, an imperial councillor, with detailed terms of reference and procedure drawn up by Aleander. The delegates were to make every effort to convey their mission to Frederick in person and in private. They were to emphasize that the Emperor was motivated only by zeal for the Faith and to preserve the unity of Christendom. They were to ask the prince not to allow himself to be guided by any kind of personal considerations in his own interest. Complaints about ecclesiastical abuses were not to be confused with matters of faith. The truth and worth of the Faith remain inviolate, even if those who profess it fail somewhat. Luther attacks the Popes, spiritual authority, and the papal decrees in an unheard of manner. Only the fear of punishment has caused him to refrain from the same attacks on secular authority. If the papal power were brought to nought all secular power, imperial and princely, would fall with it, for all power was derived from the Pope. Against Leo's person nobody could lay any charge. The abuses of the Roman Curia prove on closer examination to be much less serious than they were made out to be. Appropriate machinery exists to deal with them: they should be reported to the Emperor who would seek redress in Rome. The Prince must consider whether the Church could have erred for so many centuries and only Luther with his handful of supporters be in the right. Were Luther so evangelical as he claims, he could not on these religious grounds have spoken so shockingly of Popes and councils, and have created such offence by burning the papal decretals. And if Luther emphasizes (as the Prince affirmed when he was in Cologne) that he had been compelled to write in the way he had owing to the opposition of Eck and other antagonists, it would have been a far finer proof of the quality of his evangelical life, if he had not sought to destroy the Catholic Faith under such a pretext. The Prince's request to give Luther a hearing before burning his books was pointless, for Luther's writings spoke clearly enough for themselves. Moreover, Luther repudiates as judges of his cause all theologians, jurists and philosophers, and will only be heard by laity favourably disposed to him. But in matters of faith the laity, not excluding the Emperor, were not competent judges. Luther will come to the Diet on a safe conduct only if he can pour out his poison scot-free, and create the impression that the Emperor and princes approve his writings. Luther is not open to conviction on the basis of argument and authority: he will accept the New Testament only in so far as it accords with his own brand of interpretation, and what does not please him (as, for example, the Epistle of James) he dismisses as foolish. The authority of the Pope, the ceremonies of the Church and the substance of the Faith must never be dragged down into subject matter for disputation.

Moreover, it would not please the Prince if his own subjects sought to correct him and wanted to oppose him. The Prince may want to protect himself from excommunication and interdict rather than trust the Luther appeal. It is both foolish and blameworthy if Luther believes that under such a pretext he can repudiate and reject everything. Such action would not save either him or his supporters from excommunication. On the subjects of confession, the Lord's Supper and extreme unction Luther teaches other than the Church. The Prince must so bring it about, by persuasion or by force, that Luther revokes his erroneous doctrines now so widely disseminated by his writings, and the Pope will then forgive him and restore him to grace and favour. Independently of that, and it is for this reason the delegates had been specifically sent, the Prince was to have Luther's writings burnt in accordance with the Emperor's command duly promulgated in diet before the Empire. Luther himself, however, he was to hold in custody, until the Emperor in consultation with his princes and councillors in Diet, had decided what to do with him. His responsibility was to hand him over to the Emperor according to law, and it was the Emperor's responsibility to go into the matter of Luther's further prosecution in consultation with the Pope. The Prince must not demur. He could not object out of consideration of his people, for people take their lead from their Prince, and he could seek to influence them by means of preachers and councillors. If the approval and support of the Prince, boasted of by Luther in a letter to Crotus, were withdrawn, Luther's boldness would disappear with it. The will and intention of the Emperor in this matter shall be communicated and made clear to the Prince. The Emperor considers it his bounden duty not to allow such a state of affairs to come to pass, and if it did, certainly not to allow it to last for any length of time. He would use all his power and authority to forestall that eventuality. He will not refrain from the banning and the burning of Luther's writings notwithstanding what the Prince keeps on saying, that the books are condemned without giving the author a hearing. This position is untenable, as had been properly argued. Notorious errors and heresy of this kind have often been condemned by Popes and Councils without giving their authors a hearing. The argument which the Prince brought forward in Cologne, namely, that the Luther affair was being considered by Cajetan and the Archbishop of Trier and therefore the Pope could not take further proceedings while the matter was *sub judice,* is thereby refuted.

The outcome of all this will be that Luther will gain a hearing at the Diet with the purpose of submitting the authority of the Pope to the judgment of laymen and gaining approval of his actions and views with the support of enemies of the Curia. And because he knows that the papal legates will not allow this to happen, on this account he steps out in the grand manner. And even if he were given a hearing before the Diet and there condemned, in that event he would at once appeal to a general council. He would behave at the Diet exactly as he did before Cajetan at Augsburg, where he recanted on the first day but took it all back on the second day before notaries and witnesses, and on the strength of his safe conduct returned home with impunity.

A letter of Luther to his Prince, dated 25 January 1521, is

obviously a reply to one from Frederick (now lost). Presumably the Prince had spoken to the Emperor on the Luther affair soon after his arrival in Worms on 5 January requesting an impartial hearing for Luther. Frederick had received a favourable audience and an assurance that Luther would not be condemned unheard. In his reply Luther states that he is enclosing a copy of his *Protestatio* (WA. 2. 620ff) and expresses his readiness to stand before an impartial tribunal subject to the issue of a safe conduct. Luther's trust in such a piece of paper and his hopes of being received impartially were the cause of much anxiety among his more worldly (and realistic) supporters. They remembered the fate of Huss even in posssession of a safe conduct and were more aware of court intrigue. Aleander was working indefatigably, in the face of much support for Luther, to dismiss all these legal niceties and to get Luther condemned categorically and immediately. When the *Protestatio* was handed to the Emperor on the 6 February by the court marshall of Duke John of Saxony, who requested the Emperor to see that justice be done to the petitioner, the Emperor in the presence of the courtiers assembled displayed a lack of wisdom in tearing up the petition into fragments and throwing them on the floor. This conduct gave immense satisfaction to Aleander who wrote of it as 'a clear indication to the whole Diet of what the Emperor thinks of Luther', and also of how 'the Emperor holds firmly to the good cause'. Those solid Germans standing by would have their own ideas of such behaviour, and also of how much ill it augured for their cause and Luther's.

Undeterred by this unseemly exhibition Frederick insisted that Luther be given a hearing before the Diet under the imperial safe conduct. Frederick had too much support to be brushed aside, to say nothing of his own bluff integrity which could not admit any gross injustice. Even Aleander, who could rely implicitly on imperial support in executing the Papal Bull, could not turn a blind eye to the stubborn truth. He himself admitted that he was up against not a mere individual but an individual at the head of a nation. 'The whole of Germany is in revolt,' he wrote on 8 February. 'Nine people out of ten cry "Luther" and the tenth, "Death to the Roman Curia!" The entire nation is unanimous in its demand for a Council to be held on German soil.' Aleander argued that if the Papal Curia delayed any longer its action against Luther, the Lutherans would have the upper hand in Germany for they had no respect at all for any papal excommunication and soon the Imperial Council itself will be unable to issue an edict against them. The clergy will not or dare not preach against Luther. The printing presses are simply raining Luther's books every day, even here in Worms under their very eyes. Erasmus is now openly supporting Luther, and Erasmus, who carries enormous prestige, has written far worse things against the Church than Luther ever did. Aleander averred that he was afraid to appear on the streets and lived in daily fear of being murdered. Were the Emperor to falter at this fateful hour, the whole of Germany would be lost to the Roman See.

Aleander's hand was strengthened at this moment when the Pope issued his final bull of excommunication of Luther and his followers, entitled *Decet Romanum,* 3 January 1521 (p. 96). The Bull reached Aleander on 10 February 1521 and with it a papal missive to the Emperor enjoining its immediate execution. The Emperor's councillors continued to advise Charles of the importance of carrying the Diet along with him in his conduct of the Luther affair, and as a consequence Aleander was invited to address the Estates on the matter on 13 February 1521, Ash Wednesday. It was, in fact, the first official speech for the prosecution (RA. II 494–507).

Aleander, of course, spoke in Latin, and the only text of the speech we have is that of Chancellor Bruck, in German. Frederick was absent, being ill. To an audience largely hostile he spoke for three hours, quite uninhibited. Those German princes present must have endured it as a heavy penance on the first day of Lent. The English text, parts of which now follow, is a translation of the Bruck text, itself a German rendering of the original Latin speech.

Before he entered upon his main speech he delivered by way of prelude the *Apostolic Breve* of 18 January 1521, intended to be read to the Council. In this letter the Pope reminds the Emperor with reference to the Bull, *Exsurge, Domine* of 15 June 1520 how he had earlier condemned Luther's erroneous teaching and ordered his books to be burnt; but as for Luther himself he had commanded him to refrain from all preaching and disputation, to burn his books within a given time, to recant his errors and file a declaration thereof to the Pope or to appear before him under a safe conduct. Since Luther had not answered the summons the Pope had declared him and his supporters obstinate heretics, and had publicly proclaimed the Bull to this effect in Rome and ordered its promulgation in Germany. (He understood from the papal nuntio that the Emperor had given his support to this action.) The Pope entered on this course of action in the hope that Luther would take it gently and return to the bosom of Mother Church. In that Luther went from bad to worse in spite of the Pope's efforts, after due consultation and advice in the matter, the Pope had condemned the errors of Luther and his supporters, separated them from the flock as black sheep and inflicted spiritual punishment on them (by means of the Bull *Decet Romanum* on 3 January 1521). All that remained to be done now was for the secular arm to execute the mandate. The Pope then warns the Emperor to recall how keenly the earlier emperors had fought heresy, and reminds him how richly God had already blessed him in his tender youth. God had given him the chief secular sword. He would wield it in vain if he did not use it against unbelievers and heretics. On that account he adjures him to rise to this his first opportunity of showing how dearly in his heart he holds the unity and peace of Christendom, and to support the Pope in the due execution of his edicts. And further, that it be

widely proclaimed to all Christ's faithful people, the Emperor
be responsible

> for the promulgation of a general edict throughout the cities
> and land of Germany to hand over this same Martin and
> other heretics supporting him as well as those who further and
> harbour him and those who follow such perversity, to those
> punishments decreed against them in our missives, unless
> they recant. They are to be punished by ordering the rulers
> of the cities and the governors of thy provinces and all other
> public servants and officials under punishments which seem to
> thee appropriate, that it be declared and made known by
> public proclamation that they would take proceedings against
> this same Martin as well as against these condemned heretics,
> his supporters, and all who favour and further the cause,
> according to the express command of our instructions.

Aleander then turned to his main speech, which was actually
the opening speech for the prosecution in Luther's trial, although
Luther was not present to hear it. When Luther was actually
summoned to appear in court the prosecution was taken over by
Eck the court official (not the same person as Eck the disputant
of Leipzig) for Aleander refused to be in the same room with
Luther, already prejudged as a heretic.

Aleander's first point was an appeal to the Emperor to take
immediate action and bring this shameful rebellion of Luther
to an end, for already an immense amount of harm had been
done to Christendom.

To appraise the emperor, electors and princes of the problem
Aleander offered a brief summary of its history. He argued that
great commotion had been stirred up on a world-wide scale at
Luther's attempt to spread a new heresy. The Pope had summoned Luther to him to discuss the affair in a kind and fatherly
manner, but Luther had remained obdurate and contumacious.
In response to Luther's action the Pope had gone into long
deliberations with learned advisers the outcome of which was

the considered condemnation of Luther in the Bull *Exsurge, Domine*.

In promulgation of the Bull Aleander had gone to Cologne where he had been given shocking and shameful treatment. However, with the help of the authorities he did manage to organize a public bonfire of Luther's books. Following this, wild calumnies have been spread abroad to the effect that Aleander is acting venomously without the Pope's knowledge or the Emperor's approval, and that he is simply furthering his own ends, bribing officials. This he dismissed as slander, promising to submit sufficient evidence to merit the burning of 100,000 heretics.

He then turned to submit his evidence for the case against Luther. All the matter which Aleander now raises has already appeared in the summary of the Bull (p. 83ff.) and in Luther's *Defence and Explanation* (summarized p. 102–12). Here a brief summary of Aleander's presentation will suffice. He selected 13 points.

First he took a copy of Luther's *Assertio* (Luther's answer to the Pope's selection of 41 points pronounced as heretical in the Bull, (see p. 102) and read out the passage where Luther had defended Huss and condemned a General Council (Constance, 1415), but where he actually stated of himself that he had now advanced beyond his Leipzig position. Aleander states, 'He has publicly declared that all the articles which were condemned at Constance were Christian, while those which the same Council permitted and approved, were heretical. What brazen effrontery! What a sacred Council approves, Luther condemns: and what the same Council condemns, Luther reviles!'

Aleander then goes on to argue that the outcome of Luther's support of Huss displayed in his criticism of Constance has been his support of Wycliffe, both men condemned by General Council. 'Luther states that the body of God (Christ) is not really present in the sacrament of the altar under both species. O gracious God, what an outrageous slander, what a blasphemy is here spoken against Thee! With these words Luther offends and blasphemes God in heaven! Has it come to this that we have now begun to doubt how and whether God is truly present in the sacrament of the altar?' Not only does Luther repeat Wycliffe's blasphemous denial of transubstantiation but also his dangerous doctrine of the limits to the authority of the State. Aleander read an extract from Luther's *On the freedom of a Christian Man* to emphasize the grave threat to the secular establishment inherent in the Lutheran theology. 'With this article alone Luther sins against our most holy father the Pope, against your imperial majesty, and against all secular authority.'

Next Aleander referred to the subject of purgatory. Luther expresses the opinion that belief in it cannot be proved from Scripture, arguing further that there is no uniformity of view in Christendom on this topic for the Church of the East has never believed it yet nobody doubts the orthodoxy of that communion. Aleander repudiates both points in the way they are treated in the Bull.

Aleander then works through a longish list of principles and persons against whom Luther has sinned. The list includes the angels of heaven whom Luther said he would not believe if they were to come down and preach a Gospel other than Christ's; the clerical priesthood for he preaches the priesthood of all believers; the spiritual orders for he criticises the monks and nuns; all the rites and ceremonies of Christendom; the saints, whom he will not reverence and the writings of whom he criticises as legendary; the secular judges; the holy councils which he holds in disregard. Finally, he refers to Luther's doctrine of the unfree will and his teaching on indulgences but dropped both subjects immediately. In all of these points Aleander strengthened his case by reading extracts from Luther's writings which he had brought along with him.

Passing on from the enumeration of Luther's heresies Aleander spoke of the misguided support many people offered the new theology. Many are of the opinion that Luther speaks and writes evangelical truth and that he strengthens his case on the solid ground of holy scripture.

> Whether in fact Martin Luther has spoken evangelical truth in those extracts I read out to you, your Imperial Majesty, as well as the electors, princes and estates, will judge otherwise. For though he seeks to strengthen his heretical views by the occasional text from scripture, nevertheless he always quotes with an interpretation other than the holy fathers pronounced, other than the holy mother of Christendom has accepted, acknowledged and maintained. It is the technique of heretics: they seek to prove their false teaching as true by quoting scripture. The Devil can deceive men no more simply than in the likeness of a good man and under the guise of the good. The heretics behave in like manner.

It is also said that Luther is a pious man and that he leads a godly life. 'If that were so may it not be suggested that his learning should lead him to different conclusions, or that he should expound the scriptures otherwise than he understands them with his God-given gifts?' Heretics always are the smoothest of hypocrites but inwardly they are ravening wolves. 'Were we to grant that Luther leads the life of a pious and Christian man, that does not entitle him to know more than the holy fathers and the mother of Christendom have known and maintained until now.'

He went on to say that it was maintained in certain quarters that even if Luther had erred on certain points, it is surely not right to burn all his books on that account, for manifestly they contain much that is good. This school of thought gives Origen as a precedent: Origen was admittedly heretical on certain points, yet nobody wants to burn his works. His books are preserved and studied. There is no parallel, Aleander decisively avers. When Origen wrote there was no authority and no scholar to show him that he had erred. Luther has been warned many times, and though fully appraised of the situation, still persists

9 Cardinal Aleander
*From an anonymous
drawing*

10 Luther as an
Augustinian Friar, with
Doctor's cap, 1521
*From an engraving by
Lucas Cranach The Elder*

in his stubborn self-will. Further, Luther's errors are far more serious than Origen's. Here Aleander defends the practice of burning heretics and their books.

Finally, some counsel that Luther be given a safe conduct to allow a hearing of his case at this Diet now sitting at Worms, fearing, as they say, that if this hearing be not granted the Emperor would have an uprising of the people on his hands. Such a procedure is inappropriate. Luther recognizes no authority anyway.

> Had he really wanted a hearing, and had he really sought conviction, he could simply have appeared before His Holiness the Pope and had his hearing there. He was given this chance by Papal Bull, and on the assurance of a safe conduct. This is what His Holiness the Pope as a gentle father would far rather have seen happen. But, contrary to the will of the apostolic see, Martin Luther has appealed directly to a council. In the strength of his own wantonness and rebellious self-preferences it is his intention not to allow recognition of our own most holy father the Pope.

Further, the Diet is not a competent court in this matter. The Emperor himself is not in a position to judge affairs of this kind: certainly it is no matter for the laity of a lower estate. Were the Pope to go so far as to commit the matter to a competent court on German soil, and in that event were Luther not to be satisfied with its findings, he would at once appeal beyond it to the world at large. He will not accept the authority even of Church councils much less lay councils. The Diet has only one course to take:

> The very first thing to do is for your Imperial Majesty, Electors, Princes and Estates, to take the matter in hand and issue orders throughout the Empire, to the effect that, since Martin Luther has disobeyed the bull, all his books must be burnt; by means of one universal edict you will have to order

I

that henceforth his books shall not be printed, bought or sold; you will have to establish this and make it effective.

Aleander touched on most of the important theological points under dispute actually quoting from Luther's books which he had in court with him. In the course of his speech he referred to Luther's views on the authority of Councils; Luther's revival of the condemned theologies of Huss and Wycliffe; Luther's rejection of the doctrine of transubstantiation; his views on the limits of secular authority; his rejection of purgatory; his rejection of the worship of saints; his doctrine of the priesthood of all believers; his rejection of monasticism; his criticism of Catholic rites and ceremonies; his teaching on the unfree will; his repudiation of indulgences. Yet the whole speech, apart from its inherent tediousness, makes dismal reading. No point was discussed: no criticism answered. The tottering house was whitewashed and Luther ordered out. Instead of a three hours' speech Aleander might as well have uttered four words: *Roma locuta, causa finita.*

The speech was an impassioned appeal to maintain the *status quo* of Church and State against any and every change, and to silence Luther once and for all. No reference was made to the political and social evils which chafed Europe, no recognition of the grave academic and theological disquiet about to rend Europe in twain. With brazen effrontery Aleander pretended that all was well except for this self-opinionated and dangerous anarchist, Martin Luther, who, if not arrested and silenced forthwith, would destroy all constituted authority, spiritual and secular. The Pope could not have found a better advocate in all Christendom. Aleander dishonestly avoided any discussion of the points and criticisms which Luther had made. The Lutheran princes openly scowled to show their dissatisfaction, a sentiment Aleander was later to meet in the Diet when they doggedly pursued the amelioration of the scandals and abuses inflicted on Germany by the Papal Curia.

Aleander, nevertheless, had sufficient support to effect a resolution to submit the draft of an edict against Luther and his supporters to the Diet on 15 February 1521, on which a draft commission had already been at work some weeks. Aleander wanted it issued on authority of the Emperor alone without reference to the Estates, as he had already done in his Burgundy lands, lest the Estates were to tie the Emperor's hands, but Charles rightly realized the importance of carrying the Estates with him.

It is a wordy four-page indictment of Luther, for which Aleander himself was largely responsible. It begins by repeating how oft the Pope in true papal generosity and gentleness had tried to warn Luther of the errors of his unchristian, unnatural and damnable doctrines. For some time now Luther had perpetrated sermons, writings and books against the Popes, the papacy, the faith, the unity of the Church, as well as against the decrees and resolutions both of the Councils of the Church and the parliaments of secular authority, constituted by lawful authority. He has done untold harm alike to secular and spiritual government. The authorities have burned these books, or prevented their further use, so that Christian folk may follow sound Christian teaching and tradition. In utter disregard of such fatherly concern of the Pope, Luther has gone on in his own wicked, heretical, pig-headed way. Every day he seeks only to pervert and destroy the entire structure of law and righteousness, given to us and all Christian men, by our forefathers. This he does in his preaching, his writings and his books, to lead the good pious common folk into a novel and damnable maze of errors. He turns them against Pope and priesthood, both of which, mark you, were instituted by God. Finally, he seeks to incite the people against spiritual and secular authority, the outcome of which will be rebellion and bloodshed, all under the guise of spiritual truth.

The document goes on in this tautologous, magniloquent style, to describe how the Pope had taken the whole matter to heart and consulted the college of cardinals, bishops, prelates, doctors and masters of the Christian nation and called Luther before them. How Luther had obstinately gone his own way. How Luther's books had been ordered to be burnt. How Luther had had the chance to recant.

The Emperor, now, protector of the Church and bearer of the secular sword, commands obedience to the Bull. Born to this task, and desiring personally to do it, he intends to defend the faith, the decrees and resolutions of the Church and of his predecessors; to defend further the Holy Father and the papacy, to the utmost of his ability. Luther has been declared a notorious heretic. He stands condemned, and there is now no need to grant him a further hearing. Under threat of far-reaching penalties, the Emperor prohibits all buying, selling, reading, listening to or printing any of Luther's writings or books, written or not yet written. No man may discuss them, spread them, expound them, keep them or put them to any use. This was to apply throughout his domains. These poisonous and unspeakable books serve only to stir up social unrest, destroy the faith and cause widespread bloodshed, thereby destroying spiritual and secular authority. They are to be officially sought out and publicly destroyed. The Bull must be duly and properly executed. Luther, in that he has not recanted, must be arrested, kept in safe custody, to be handed over to us, or held until it has been decided what to do with him. Luther's supporters and abettors of whatever status or rank are to have the same treatment: their life, their property and their goods are to be forfeited. Any subject disobeying this decree in any way whatever will be guilty of high treason (RA. II 509–13).

This statement produced a furore in the Diet. In the electoral chamber Joachim of Brandenburg and Frederick of Saxony almost came to blows and had to be separated one from another in the ensuing brawl, while the normally taciturn Ludwig V 'roared like a bull' in support of Frederick's protest. By the 19 February they had produced their reply, a highly responsible document, correct, constitutional and courteous. The mood and mind of Germany—and much of Europe—is couched in this declaration (RA. II 514–17).

They declared that they had studied the draft, and that they offered general support to the Emperor, but hoped that he would heed their views in this matter.

The Estates had taken counsel together and had debated and discussed the document with care. They expressed admiration for the gracious concern of his Christian Majesty, not only for the German people but for the whole of Christendom.

First, the Emperor must know that throughout the length and breadth of Germany the man in the street at the present time thinks of nothing else but Luther's preaching, teaching and writings. What purpose would it now serve to declare that Luther was to be silenced unheard, except to create rebellion and disturbance?

Secondly, the mandate would produce uncertainty. The people would want to know whether in fact Luther had been cited and where he was to appear; whether he was to be given a further hearing or not. It is the considered opinion of the Estates that Luther be heard before competent and impartial judges, under a safe conduct. The Estates should seek to ascertain (though not in the form of a disputation), whether Luther stands by the writings and articles which he has published against our holy, Christian Faith, the Faith we and our forefathers have held to this day. He must be asked whether he persists in them or not.

Were Luther to recant to this extent, he should be granted a further hearing on those points and matters bearing on the reform of the Church, and these could be set right. On the other hand, if he insists on all those articles, or perhaps most of those which are against the Christian Church and the holy Catholic Faith—the Faith which we, our fathers and our forebears have believed and maintained until now—and if he persists in holding his views, then in that event all the electors, princes and other estates of the Holy Empire stand alongside and behind the Holy Roman Emperor. They stand by the Faith of their fathers and forefathers and hold the articles of the Christian Faith without further debate. They pledge their support to the Faith, and their loyalty to the Emperor in respect of all mandates and orders constitutionally issued throughout the Empire.

There is one further point. The Estates beg his Imperial Majesty, as their most gracious Lord and Emperor of Rome, to bear in mind the gravity and importance of the matter, and to heed the warning the Estates are now giving. They beg him to handle the matter in such a way as to bring good to the entire German nation, to the Holy Roman Empire, to our Christian Faith and to all estates and members of the same.

> The estates of the Empire bring all this to the further attention and pleasure of your Imperial Majesty. In doing so we make one final request, in loyalty and obedience: that your Imperial Majesty will of his graciousness bear in mind the nature of the grievances and scandals which now lie upon the Empire and which very largely stem from Rome. And in bearing them in mind, graciously investigate these affairs so that the scandals be taken from us and matters set to rights.

There is no mistaking the burden of this document as courageous as it was clear. It was a warning to the Emperor and to the world of how everybody was now alerted to the perilous spiritual, social, political and economic unrest in Europe. These matters would now no longer be settled by authoritarian declaration. The common man was aware of the situation and demanded justice and truth. He was also aware of the grave responsibility the Church of Rome had for this state of affairs and he now demanded effective reformation. The discerning reader will notice how bitterly Rome resented this new lay and democratic power arising in Europe and how often the blame for it was laid at Luther's door. Aleander knew that if Luther were ever given a hearing the seat of power would move from Peter to people. Posterity owes much to this stand of the lay

princes in the cause of common justice. Be that as it may, the estates baulked Aleander in his high-handed ecclesiastical attempt to promulgate the edict without reference to lay opinion and scotched his persistent cunning in refusing to recognize the clamant need for a reformation. Admittedly, the Estates had not the conception entailed in Reformation as Luther saw it, but they did maintain a situation in which Luther was given of protection. At all events he did get a trial of sorts.
some sort of hearing and which afforded him a limited kind

The document also caused a change in imperial policy. The Emperor called the estates to discuss the Luther affair with him on Friday 1 March 1521 at 4 p.m. with particular reference to three questions. One, at what place and at what time Luther should be cited: presumably, not far from the Emperor. Secondly, the Emperor thought the estates had made a good point when they argued that though Luther's sermons, writings and books contained articles manifestly contrary to holy Faith and to Christian teaching, there was no point now in burning or otherwise destroying these books, after they had already disseminated their errors all over the place. Thirdly, were Luther to stay away and refuse to present himself within a given time under a safe conduct, or were he to appear and refuse to recant, he would then be declared a notorious heretic, arrested, and prosecuted. This is but the bounden duty of his Imperial Majesty as Emperor of Rome, in fulfilling which he hopes to have the support of the Estates of the Empire as well as their subjects.

The next day, 2 March, a written statement was given to the Estates by the Emperor as a reply to their submission of 19 February with reference to an edict against Luther, his hearing, and the catalogue of grievances against Rome.

The Emperor first thanked the Electors, Princes and Estates for their responsible reply as Christian leaders concerned for the welfare of the Empire, the German nation, the Christian Church and for the Faith. The whole world was indebted to them and would express its thanks.

His Majesty graciously approved their advice that Luther be required to appear, to be examined, and to be given a hearing. That he be asked to recant what he has preached, written and published against our Sacred Faith. That in the event of Luther's refusal they would straightway stand with and behind the Emperor in support of their traditional Faith without any further disputation.

The Emperor has accepted their advice and learned counsel, and will require Luther to appear under a safe conduct there and back, as outlined above and as expressed in the letter appended.*

Finally, in that the electors, princes and estates desire the Emperor to look into the grievances and abuses which lie so heavily on the Holy Roman Empire and which may be largely blamed upon the papacy, the Emperor is well disposed to consider these complaints and requests that their representations be put into writing when he would discuss them with the Electors, Princes and Estates, kindly and sympathetically.

The second draft referred to in this letter had been drawn up under considerable difficulties for which there exists only Aleander's reports. On receipt of the letter from the estates on 19 February the Emperor convoked his councillors who, though they sat up till ten o'clock at night, failed to reach a common mind. The Emperor then appointed a commission to go further into the matter, consisting of the Bishops of Salzburg, Sitten, Triest, Palencia, Tuy, his father confessor Glapion (excluded from the recent commissions), and three doctors. The Archbishop of Salzburg made it clear to Aleander that he was personally against Luther's appearance at the Diet, but because the princes had settled for it, they could not go back on that decision at this stage. Aleander remained steadfast to the papal cause and was its vigilant protagonist, but both Chièvres and Gattinara informed him that the princes had made it clear to the Emperor that they would not obey a mandate that had

*The second draft of the edict dated 10 March 1521.

been drawn up in any other way. The Archbishop of Salzburg undertook to re-draft it in such a way that the princes would raise no objection and Aleander would accept, though deliberately keeping Aleander out of the deliberations. Though not a member of the commission Aleander was very active behind the scenes in deep concern lest the initiative be taken out of the hands of Rome and taken by laymen.

The second draft covered the same ground in essentials as the first. The whole story was recapitulated but sweeping and severe statements of Luther's theology and conduct were made, prefaced by the tale of the wonderful forgiving forbearance of the Pope who in his gentle and fatherly way had ever sought to win Martin. Luther was charged with destroying the Holy Catholic Faith and the unity of the Church; he sought to abolish the holy decretals, the decrees and Church councils, authoritative for centuries; he despises law and order; he leads the common people astray into novelty and damnable error; he seeks to destroy the holy sacraments and traditional Christian teaching; he is against the Holy Father, the papacy, all spiritual and temporal authority; he restores the heresies of Wycliffe and Huss, long condemned by Pope, Emperor and Church Council at Constance 1415, and actually called that Council a conference of devils presided over by the Antichrist; he has burnt books, decrees, decretals and much other approved Christian learning; he seeks to lead the common people on, not only in a novel, perverted, damnable insolence, but towards a serious deterioration of authority. The same kind of conditions were made for Luther to retract as were in the first draft, but no mention made of the important request of the Estates whereby if Luther retracted in whole or in part, the Diet should go on to discuss the reform of abuses. Still worse, the proposed edict demanded that Luther's books be burned together with all his vile unchristian sermons and other writings, an edict covering even all those of his supporters and well-wishers; that these books be no more bought or sold, accepted or put to any use;

that they be no more written or printed, nor their contents supported or upheld. Disobedience would incur the utmost severity of both canon and civil law.

The document, compromise though it is, provoked heated discussion and failed to secure the approbation of the Estates. The latter asked the Emperor for four to five days to discuss it, but he felt he could allow them only until five o'clock that day. They produced their answer by 5 p.m., an answer now lost but presumably on the lines of their previous statement. This was given to the Emperor at 8 a.m. on 6 March. The summons to Luther and the letter of safe conduct are dated 6 March, and no doubt negotiations with the Estates were concluded that same day. According to Aleander the Mandate seems to have been completed by 8 March. Aleander took the credit upon himself that the Mandate retained a form in accordance with the dignity and intentions of the Pope. By 11 March Aleander was awaiting the completion of the printing and on 17 or 18 March it was completed, but it was only on 26 March that it was posted and on 27 March proclaimed. By that time the Emperor had renounced the cooperation of the Estates and published it without further reference to them. This means that the document was issued on the authority of the Emperor alone without the support of the Diet, though Brieger takes the view that there had been virtual cooperation in all but the final stage. The Germans, as a whole, took the view that the responsibility for both the summons as well as the safe conduct was the Emperor's and nobody else's, nevertheless, the Saxons disapproved its issuance as a breach of faith.

The citation (RA. II 526–7) is couched in terms in striking contrast with those of the edict. It runs:

Worms, 6 March 1521

Charles, by the grace of God elected Holy Roman Emperor, Caesar Augustus of the Empire etc. . . .
Honourable, dear, and reverend Sir,

Inasmuch as We and the Estates of the Holy Roman Empire, now assembled here, have undertaken and decided to receive some explanation from you on account of the doctrines and books which you have produced for some time now, We give you immediate security and a safe conduct to come to Us here, and from here a safe return home, a safe conduct recognized by Us and our Empire and attached herewith; We do this with the earnest desire that you will forthwith arise and come to Us, and within twenty-one days be with Us here for certain, nothing doubting. Do not stay aloof: you need have no anxiety on the score of violence or injustice. It is Our intention to deal with you in strict accordance with the aforementioned safe-conduct. We eagerly await your arrival on these terms. Take this as our earnest intention.

Given in Worms our imperial city on the sixth day of the month of March in the year of our Lord 1521 and in the second year of our reign.

The Elector followed this up on 11 March with his own safe conduct to see Luther through his own territory and that of his brother. The delay was owing to the Emperor's insistence that the Elector should cite Luther, and Frederick's refusal, on the ground that an imperial summons would have the official weight of the whole Diet behind it, while his own citation would carry only his own individual authority.

To Aleander the imperial decision was a gross error. The Church could have no truck with a notorious heretic and the plain duty of the Emperor and of the Diet was not to hear him but to execute without question the papal condemnation. He was apprehensive of Luther's appearance before the Diet, and saw no good in permitting Luther to speak: 'If Luther comes, you can fear the worst,' he remarked with foreboding. It was this fear that made him press for the publication of the edict against Luther's writings without the approbation of the Estates. This he succeeded in achieving, when the edict was promulgated in the name of the Emperor on 27 March, though in a modified form. His hope was that Luther would see that the Diet had already made up its mind and that there was little point in making an appearance after all.

While all this was going on Luther simply worked at his task and waited on his God. In a letter to a friend he writes, aware of his many foes, 'Pray the Lord for me, that I may think and speak and write what becomes both Him and me, though not them.' And when Staupitz deserted him, exhorting him to humility and warning him against the sin of pride and arrogance, Luther replied that if he had shown too much arrogance, his adviser had shown too much humility. Staupitz in his surrender to Antichrist in condemning Luther had condemned Christ and was no better than a deserter. Had not Christ given Himself for us, Luther argued, ought we not to fight and give our life for him? 'More is at stake in this matter than many are aware of: the Gospel is involved.' He said that he had been accused of every kind of vice, not only arrogance, but there was one sin of which he would never be convicted: an unholy silence while he watched Christ being crucified again. The Word of Christ is not always the word of peace, but the word of the sword. If Staupitz cannot follow, he might at least let Luther forge ahead. 'By the grace of Christ I will not keep silent.' 'The hand of God not of man is still clearly on this matter, and to this faith I will cling in spite of the raging floods and tumults against which I am battling and which are sweeping me along.'

On 26 March the imperial herald rode into Wittenberg and up to the door of the Black Cloister to deliver to Luther in person the impressive imperial citation with its weighty seals. The pomp and dignity with which the summons was carried out, and the high-sounding and courteous language in which the citation is written, implied at least that Charles knew the importance of the man he was summoning and the weight of the issues concerned. Charles actually sent his own imperial herald, Caspar Sturm, a member of a distinguished Rhine family, and a man critical of the papalists and certainly well disposed to Luther. All this added a lot of colour and eclat to the occasion, and the town authorities busily organized a wagon, horses and a fund for expenses. Luther waited until the Easter services were over, continued writing his books, and then quietly set out on 2 April, Easter Tuesday, with the citation, the safe-conduct and his prince's official documents in his pocket and three friends on the cart—Nicholas Amsdorf, the theologian, John Petzensteiner, a brother monk, and Peter Suaven, a young student. The people stopped work and watched the little procession wend southwards over the Elbe—with much wondering in their minds, and with deep pride and emotion for their professor.

Luther journeyed through Leipzig, Weimar, Erfurt, Gotha, Eisenach, Frankfurt, Oppenheim to Worms, preaching on the way. Many warned him not to proceed, for his fate would be the same as Huss. In several towns he saw the imperial edict posted up, an attempt by Aleander to scare him into retreat. At Oppenheim, the crafty father confessor of the Emperor, Glapion, hatched a last-minute plot using Bucer as the messenger, in an attempt to persuade Luther to turn aside to the Ebernburg and settle the whole matter away from the publicity of the Diet, which in any case, was a highly unsuitable court. The effect of this would have been that Luther's case would have gone by default and his imperial safe conduct would have lapsed, an outcome Aleander and the papalists were very anxious to see. Luther answered firmly, 'If Glapion wants to speak to me, he can do so at Worms,' and added that they could expect anything from him—except flight and recantation. He repeated his famous remark made when the imperial herald saw the first copy of the imperial edict and looking into the cart asked Luther if he wanted to go on, 'even if there were as many devils in Worms as there are tiles on the roofs, I would enter anyway'. He journeyed on 'in mere simplicity of heart' as he described it, and entered Worms on Tuesday 16 April 1521 at 10 a.m., a journey of fourteen days, about 250 miles.

Luther arrived in a Worms different from the Wittenberg he had left, a Worms indicative of the coarse irreligion of his day. The reading of the documents in the *Reichstagsakten* (Vol. 2. 233ff) is dismal. There were colourful and costly wares in the shops, wealth boasted on the streets, and gluttonous, gargantuan indulgence in the taverns. There was jousting in the fields by day and drinking in the inns by night. An observer wrote of leading prelates spending most of their time banqueting and drinking (Lent though it was) and of one prelate who lost 60,000 guilders at one sitting. Murders averaged three and four per night, executions for murder so far, one hundred. 'It goes on here quite as in Rome, with murdering, stealing; all the streets are full of whores; there is no Lent here, but jousting, whoring, eating of meat, mutton, pigeons, eggs, milk and cheese, and there are such doings as in the mountain of Dame Venus.'

Luther entered the town in company with a great number of nobles who had come to meet him, together with a hundred horsemen. Two thousand people awaited him. As he entered his lodgings he glanced at the crowd, which ever remembered the deep black flash of his falcon eyes. He was heard to say to himself as he stepped down from the cart, 'God will be with me.' And God was.

On the next morning Luther heard the confession of a knight who lay dying and granted him the sacrament. Informed that he was to appear before the Diet at four o'clock, he went for a hair-cut to have his tonsure clearly defined. He was then taken to the palace by a devious route owing to the throng of people.

After a wait of two hours, he was brought in to that august assembly in the packed and suffocating hall. The members of the Diet were astounded at the appearance of a slender, emaciated, pale monk of some 40 years of age. Luther had arrived in Worms only the day before, both tired and ill, and stood under very great strain. It was not only the pale, tired figure that disenchanted them. There was no panache about Luther, no pose, no pathos. The Spaniards and Italians were aghast at the plain, simple appearance of the man, quiet, with head bowed: as a monk he kept his head bowed, and when addressed gave the accustomed curtsey by bending his knees before his 'betters'. But men like this judged by outward appearances not inward realities, the way of the world.

The Trial 17–18 April 1521

There are many reports of the trial emanating from both sides of the dispute. It is encouraging to a historian to realize how closely similar these accounts are, most of them actually recorded *verbatim*. The reader will observe the varying emphasis of the different versions, yet the most careful scrutiny reveals no fact denied and none viciously misrepresented, whichever document we study. The standards of reportage are of the quality of Hansard, far in advance of any trial of today emanating from behind the iron curtain or the Middle East. All the accounts are printed in *Deutsche Reichstagsakten* Vol. 2, and a selection of them in the *Weimarer Ausgabe* Vol. 7, p. 814–882. In addition there is a list of other reports critically summarized in WA. 7. 882–887.

The main report (29 pages) is what is generally known as the Spalatin report, compiled by Spalatin, the secretary of Frederick the Wise, together with the help of the Wittenberg theologians (RA. II. 540–69). There is also an abbreviated version of this report (RA. II. 569–86), which in the nature of the case adds nothing to our knowledge of the trial. The third account (RA. II. 587–94) is the official Roman Catholic account of the trial compiled largely by the lawyer von Eck, the official prosecuting counsel, and approved by Aleander. This report is crucial to our knowledge of the trial and is here described as the Aleander— von Eck report. The fourth account (RA. II. 599–611), here named the German Report, is an anonymous account of the trial, which is friendly to Luther, and which though offering no further light on the main issues, does in fact offer a good deal of interesting procedural detail as well as many references to the personalities involved, in particular, the Archbishop of Trier, Glapion, Vehus, Cochlaeus, Schurff, Amsdorf, Peutinger. There are two further valuable reports of the proceedings, devoted mainly to the week of intense activity following the closure of the trial (see p. 164). The first of these, the Vehus report (RA. II. 611–24), is a valuably objective account, non-theological, written by a layman who was a lawyer, chancellor of the Elector Philip von Baden. It is a 5,000 word document devoted to the proceedings of 24–25 April. The other is the Cochlaeus report (RA. II. 624–632), a very valuable report, hostile to Luther. It was written by a Catholic theologian of considerable ability, present throughout the trial and a participant in the commissions called immediately after to effect some settlement. It is the only hostile account we have which is aware of the theological issues involved, and is particularly valuable not only on both accounts, but for its frank detail of the personalities engaged. It is concerned mainly with the discussions called by the Archbishop of Trier and those engaged in by Cochlaeus on his own initiative.

The procedure here is to report verbatim the main account of the trial (The Spalatin Report) and to insert interesting detail and differences which emerge from the hostile Aleander—von Eck report. This will provide a flowing account of the trial in the words of the contemporary reports, with comment from both sides. For the commissions after the trial we shall summarize the Vehus and Cochlaeus reports. The author has not chosen to give the six accounts of the trial one after the other, but the student of the period may read them if he follows up the references.

The following were present at the trial:

Charles V, Holy Roman Emperor, President.
The Electors:
Frederick, Herzog of Saxony

Charles V
om the painting by Jan van Orley

Joachim, Margrave of Brandenburg
Ludwig, Pfalzgraf of the Rhine
Albert, Archbishop of Mainz
Reinhart, Archbishop of Trier
Hermann, Archbishop of Cologne
The majority of all the other members of the Diet, princes and
gentlemen, lords secular and spiritual (with the notable excep-
tion of Cardinal Aleander who had contumaciously excepted
himself).
Ulrich von Pappenheim, Marshal of the Empire
Caspar Sturm, the imperial herald
Six Wittenberg doctors of theology
Counsel for the Prosecution:
Johann von Eck, legal officer to the Archbishop of Trier, here
as public orator for Charles V, deputizing for Aleander.
The Defendant:
Martin Luther, Professor of Biblical Studies, University of
Wittenberg.
According to the list of participants given in the *Reichstagsakten*
(RA. II. 954ff) there must have been about 1,500 all told.
All reporters speak of the packed hall and the suffocating heat.
The Spalatin Report begins:*
On the third day after Misericordias Domini Sunday (16 April),
in the year of our Lord 1521, Doctor Martin Luther, Augustinian monk by profession, travelled to Worms where he had
been summoned by Emperor Charles V, King of Spain, Archduke of Austria ... who in the first year of his reign held his
first royal court in this city. Three years earlier Doctor Martin
had proposed certain propositions for debate at Wittenberg, a
town in Saxony. These theses were directed against the tyranny
of the Bishop of Rome. Since then they had been attacked by
many, even consigned to the flames, but never confuted on the
grounds of Scripture or reason. The affair began to tend towards

*For the rest of this chapter, and in the next, verbatim quotations appear
as ordinary text; comments by the author are in italics.

rebellion, for the people were in favour of the cause of the Gospel against the clerics. On account of this it seemed a good thing, on the suggestion of the Roman legates, for the man to be summoned by an imperial herald, and letters of safe conduct given him by the Emperor and the princes to this end. He was summoned. He came, and stayed at the houses of the knights and nobles, both ecclesiastical and lay.

On the day after his arrival, the fourth day after Misericordias Domini Sunday, 17 April, Ulrich von Pappenheim, a nobleman of gentle birth and master of the imperial cavalry, was sent by the Emperor. He came before lunch and showed to Doctor Martin the mandate of Charles, by which he was to appear at four o'clock in the afternoon before His Imperial Majesty, the electoral princes, the dukes and the rest of the orders of the Empire. This, Ulrich declared, was the purpose of his visit, and Martin courteously accepted the invitation, as was his duty.

As the hour struck four on that day, Ulrich von Pappenheim came and with him Caspar Sturm, imperial herald of all Germany, the man who had summoned Doctor Martin at Wittenburg and had brought him as far as Worms. These two men invited him and accompanied him through the garden of the house of the Knights of Rhodes into the quarters of the Count Palatine. And lest he suffer in any way at the hands of the mob which had gathered in vast hordes on the usual route to the imperial residence, he came to the audience chamber by way of some back gardens unknown to the multitude. Many however did spot him and they could hardly be kept back from forcing an entry. Many climbed on to the roofs in their eagerness to catch a glimpse.

When at last he stood in the presence of His Imperial Majesty, the princes, the electors and the dukes, in short, all the orders of the Empire then in attendance upon the Emperor, Doctor Martin was warned by Ulrich von Pappenheim not to speak unless asked.

At that point Johann von Eck, public orator of His Imperial

Majesty, general secretary of the Bishop of Trier, pronounced the following statement, first in Latin and then in German:

His Imperial Majesty has summoned you here in this court for two reasons. First, that you may here in this court publicly acknowledge if the books spread abroad in your name up till now are actually yours. Then, if you confess that they are, whether you admit that they are all your own work, or whether you wish to retract any part of them.

Thereupon Doctor Jerome Schurff, a Swiss from St Gall, who stood at Martin's side, called out aloud, 'Let the titles of the books be read out.'

Thereupon the secretary of the Bishop of Trier read out one by one the names of those books of Doctor Martin which had been printed in one edition at Basel. Among these were the following, *Commentaries on the Psalms, On Good Works,* and a *Commentary on the Lord's Prayer.* Besides these there were other books of a non-controversial kind.

Aleander had actually furnished Eck with a much longer list of books, a list found in the Vatican library. It runs:
1. *Books of Martin Luther in German. 'On Good Works', 'On the Liberty of a Christian Man', 'Address to the German Nobility', 'On the New Testament and the Mass', 'An Assertion of the Articles of Luther recently condemned', 'To the Official at Stolpen', 'Appeal for a Council', 'Book against Emser', 'How to Confess', 'Sermon on Usury', 'Against Bock', 'On the Papacy at Rome'.*
2. *Latin. First Editition of 'Works' printed in Basel. 'The Babylonian Captivity', 'An Assertion of the Articles', 'On Good Works', 'Explanation of Lord's Prayer', 'An Appeal for a Council', 'Why the Books of the Pope were burned', 'Sermon in preparation of death', 'Exposition of Psalms 1–13', 'Against the Execrable Papal Bull'.*

The attention of the reader is drawn to the greater detail as well as the very much sharper form of the prosecution given by Aleander–von Eck:

> Martin Luther, His Holy and Invincible Imperial Majesty, in consultation with all the Estates of the Holy Roman Empire has ordered you to be called hither to the throne of His Majesty to retract the books which you have edited and spread abroad. I refer to all the books written in either German or Latin, and the contents of the same. Further, he has called you to retract the violence, the form and the tenor of them, in accordance with the aforementioned mandate brought against you by His Imperial Majesty and properly charged against you by lawful decree. Wherefore, I ask you in the name of His Imperial Majesty and of the princes of the Empire: First, do you confess that these books exhibited here —a bundle of his books and writings in Latin and in German were shown to him at this point—now named publicly to you one by one, and which have gone the rounds with your name on the title page, are in fact yours. Do you acknowledge these books as yours, or not? Next, do you wish to retract and recall them and their contents? Or do you want rather to cling to them and persist in them?

Since this question consisted of two parts, and Luther saw it as two questions, he answered the first part of the question. He said that the books shown to him, the titles of which had just been read out, and which were written in Latin and in German, were his, and published at his home. He admitted they were his offspring and would always acknowledge them as such. He added in a somewhat lower tone, though clearly heard, that there were others which had not been named but which were his. To the second part of the question, whether he wished to retract these aforementioned books and their contents and recant them, he began to make excuses and to contrive evasions. He said that he was prepared to yield to and agree with anyone seeking to inform him from Holy Scripture. Up till then that had not happened to him, though he had made that offer over and over again. Further, it was about a difficult and tough question, possibly the hardest of all questions, since it concerned faith. For these reasons he could not give an answer on the spur of the moment without time to reflect. On that account he asked most humbly that time for deliberation be given and allowed him.

While these things were being done and the decision implemented, His Holy Imperial Majesty, in agreement with and in counsel with all the Electors and other princes, ecclesiastical as well as lay, and of the Estates of the Empire present in great numbers, immediately expressed a wish. He wanted Luther to be told at the outset, kindly and gently, through the good offices of the aforesaid John von Eck, to keep always before his eyes the unity of the Holy Catholic and Apostolic Church, and the general peace and quiet of Christendom. That Luther should not be ready to tear apart what he ought to uphold, venerate and adore. That Luther should not be willing to rely on his own private opinion and on Biblical texts perverted by all kinds of doctrines to fit in with his own ideas. That he should not be willing to wander freely in the area of his own discoveries and those of other scholars, to overthrow the universal Christian religion, to incite the world, to confuse the lowest with the loftiest, and to seduce so many godly minds and souls. Further, Luther should now consider seriously to what extent he is already inextricably involved in his own errors. How difficult it is, nay impossible, to put them to rights again. What is more, how many souls has his self-assured spirit unhappily seduced to their dire peril and loss, how many sent to hell. What Luther needs, therefore, is to return to his senses and get back to the heart of the faith. He needs to acknowledge his errors and recant. If Luther were to do this, His Majesty for his part promised his grace and favour, and that he would readily obtain those favours on his behalf from His Holiness the Pope. If, on the other hand, he were to persevere wilfully in his errors and did not care to accept this sound advice, His Majesty now wished his own position to be declared publicly before decisions were promulgated. He for his part would defend the dignity of his own throne as well as that of the Holy Apostolic See according to law. He would do that in support of the Faith, for his whole life had been bound up with Holy Mother Church and he was obligated to the Christian religion. Luther ought to turn over in his mind what pain and punishment would ensue afterwards, and what end awaited him.

Luther has gone so far as to seek an opportunity for further consideration of the second half of the question, yet he had no right at all to make this request, nor for that matter does he deserve this preferential treatment. The nature and circumstances of the matter about which he is so concerned had already been brought to his attention. Even in the earlier mandate issued against him, a revocation which had to be made by him of his words specifically and by name, as well as their contents, was expressly written into the document.* On those grounds, because he has known for a long time to what purpose he was summoned and what was on the agenda of the Diet he should not set out to drag the matter on with further delay, particularly as it is fraught with such danger and is an exceptional matter, outside the run of customary cases. What is more he ought to have finished his deliberation on this important matter before he appeared in this court. Nevertheless, to obviate the complaint that action had been taken against Luther in far too hasty a manner, His Majesty graciously wishes to grant the deliberation requested. To this end His Majesty's wishes it to be made known that at His command he has appointed the next day following at five o'clock in the afternoon to consider and clarify the deliberation. This was to be done in like manner as His Majesty had set and appointed that present day and hour to deal with the agenda set before the Diet.

*Not so, in fact. No mention of revocation was made. See p. 131 for the document in question.

The request for time for deliberation was a very clever move on Luther's part. When the Roman party realized that Luther was to appear, they went to great pains so to prepare the questions that Luther would not be able to make any statement of his position. Further, they wanted from him a retraction. Failing that, and just as disquieting in the eyes of the public, a partial retraction. Luther, for his part, had been prudently counselled to play for time, and to see first how his prosecuting counsel was to open the case. Luther did not enjoy the support of a defence counsel as we know the term, a man who would protect his client against unjust, sinister, leading questions in the first place, and then finally open out the measure of his client before the full court. Aleander had prepared the questions for von Eck so as to prevent Luther from making any justifying statement and to wrest from him a recantation, in whole or in part. It is to Luther's lasting credit that overwhelmed with the stifling heat, utterly ill and exhausted, overawed as monk, countryman and scholar before the might and splendour of the Empire, he saw without prompting, that the manoeuvres were meant to give the outward appearance of a constitutional hearing without providing any at all. The request for time for thought dumbfounded the court. Luther's short answers and humble request showed the papal party what to expect, impressed the princes and laity of the integrity of the man, and gave Luther one quiet night to pray and think over what he was going to say.

When the orator had said this Martin was led back to his lodgings by the imperial herald. In this trial, what happened between his departure at the bidding of the Emperor and his appearance in the assembly of the princes proper, ought not to be overlooked. Luther was exhorted by many in all kinds of advice to be strong and of a good courage, to play the man, not to fear those who can only kill the body but cannot kill the soul, but to fear Him rather Who is able to cast both body and soul into Hell (Matt. 10.28). Or again, when you stand before kings, take no thought on what you should say, for it will be given to you in that hour (Luke 12.11, 12). One of those standing by cried out, Blessed is the womb that bare thee (Luke 11.27).*

All night long Luther wrestled with his problem. He was alone, for Aleander threatened death on all his friends, none of whom had a permit to be in Worms, all of whom were actually banned and excommunicated by papal bull. They fled into hiding. Luther knew it was not only Worms but the world which was watching and waiting. He also knew, what hardly occurs to contemporary man, that God was watching and waiting: that God had called him to this hour and for this hour, and that at this hour he must acquit himself as God willed, as His chosen servant. Of that momentous and memorable vigil, he has left some jottings on paper, the manuscript of which we still possess.

The Spalatin report resumes:

At four o'clock in the afternoon of the following day, the fifth day after *Misericordias Domini* Sunday, 18 April, the herald came and picked up Doctor Martin and led him off to the court of the Emperor, where he was kept waiting until six o'clock on account of the pressure of work which involved the princes. Luther had to wait in a great throng of people and became utterly exhausted with the crowds.

When the assembly was eventually called to order, Martin stood in the midst. The public orator held forth in the words following:

His Imperial Majesty has provided this occasion for you, Martin Luther, seeing that you publicly admitted that the books, which were named yesterday, were yours. Furthermore, on the question of whether you wished to disown any of them,

---

* He was later to write: 'In the meantime many of the nobility came to my lodging and said, "Herr Doctor, how is it all going? They are all saying, They want to burn you. But that must never happen. They would first have to dispose of all of us." "They would have done that as well",' was Luther's grim but realistic reply.

or whether you approved all you had published, you requested time for deliberation. That time has now run out, although by law you had no right to seek a period for further reflection. You had plenty of time to know why you were summoned. And further, it is surely a generally accepted principle that everybody should be able to give certain and unshakeable reasons for his views, whenever he is asked, not least of all a person such as you, a learned and distinguished professor of theology. Get on with it! Answer the Emperor's question. You have already experienced his kindness when you requested time for further deliberation. Do you wish to defend all the books you acknowledged as your own? Or, do you wish to retract any? This the orator said in Latin and German, more offensively in the Latin than in the German.

Doctor Martin replied, he, too, both in Latin and German. He spoke humbly, quietly and modestly, though not without the spirit and determination becoming to a Christian man, so much so in fact, that his enemies would have preferred a speech and spirit struck in a lower key. These were keenly anticipating a recantation, some hope of which they had conceived when Luther asked for time to consider.

> *The Speech of Martin Luther before the*
> *Emperor Charles and the Princes at Worms*
> *on the Fifth Day after Misericordias*
> *Domini (18 April)*

Most serene Lord Emperor, most illustrious Princes, most clement Lords.

Obedient to the time set for me yesterday evening I appear before you, beseeching you by the mercy of God, that your most serene Majesty and your most illustrious lordships may graciously be disposed to attend to this my cause, a cause which is, I hope, one of righteousness and truth. If through my inexperience I have not given the proper titles to some, or if I have offended in any way the etiquette and protocol of the court, be kind enough to overlook such faults, for I am a man at home in the cell of a monk not the courts of kings. I am able to testify no more about myself than this: up to this moment I have taught and written with a simplicity of heart that had in view only the glory of God and the sound instruction of Christ's faithful people.

Most serene Emperor, most illustrious Princes, I refer to those two questions put to me yesterday on behalf of your most sacred majesty, namely, whether I acknowledged the books published in my name and recounted in court yesterday as my own, and whether I persisted in their defence or wanted to retract them. To the first question I gave my immediate and complete answer, in which I still persist and shall persist forever Namely, these books are mine and were published by me and in my own name. Unless by some chance it has so happened that through the cunning or perhaps indiscretion of my emulators something in them has been altered or mistakenly cut out since they left my hands. Obviously, I cannot acknowledge anything except what is mine alone and written by me alone, to the complete exclusion of the assiduity of anybody else whatever.

In replying to the second question I ask that your Most Serene Majesty and your lordships may deign to consider that my books are not all of the same kind.

In some of my books I have considered religious piety and morals in such a simple and evangelical manner that even my enemies would be compelled to admit that these books are useful, innocuous, and clearly fit for Christians to read. Even the Bull [*Exsurge, Domine,* 15 June 1520], vicious and cruel though it is, maintains that some of my books are innocuous, yet even so it permits that these be condemned with an utterly monstrous judgment. If in terms of your request I should begin to disavow them, I ask you, what would I in fact be doing? Would not I, alone of all men, be condemning that very truth which friends and foes alike confess? I would be standing a solitary figure in opposition to a harmonious confession shared by all men.

There are books of another kind which inveigh against the

papacy and the goings on of the papists. These books assail them as men who both by their doctrines as well as the disgraceful example of their lives have utterly laid waste the Christian world with evil both of the spirit and the flesh. This fact none can deny or conceal. The experience of everybody and the complaints of the whole world bear witness that through the decrees of the Pope and the all too human doctrines of men the consciences of the faithful have been most wretchedly ensnared, harassed and butchered. Further, property and possessions, especially in this illustrious land of Germany, have been devoured by an unbelievable tyranny, and are being devoured unceasingly in a most shocking manner. And yet the papists by their own decrees [as in Dist. IX and XXV qu. 1 and 2]* warn that papal laws and doctrines which are contrary to the Gospel and the teachings of the Fathers must be held as erroneous and reprehensible. If therefore I retract these writings, it would be tantamount to supplying strength to this tyranny, and to opening not only windows but even doors to such great godlessness. It would spread far and wide and would increase more freely than ever before. If I were to make a recantation of this kind before the law, their kingdom of licentious and unrestrained faithlessness will become still more intolerable for the wretched populace. Their tyranny would be so much the more strengthened and secured, especially if it got around that this had been done by me on the authority of your most sacred and serene Majesty and of the entire Holy Roman Empire. Good God! Then I myself would be a shield to iniquity and tyranny.

There is a third kind of book which I have written against certain private, and as they call them, distinguished individuals. These are they who endeavour to maintain the Roman tyranny and to destroy the piety taught by me. Against these I confess I have been more severe than befits my religion or my profession. But then I do not set myself up as a saint. It is not my life I am arguing about, but the teaching of Christ. It is not right for

*Corp. jur. cod., ed. Friedberg I.16ff and 1007ff.

me to retract these works, because this very retraction would again bring about a state of affairs where tyranny and impiety would rule and rage among the people of God more violently than they ever ruled before.

However, because I am a man and not God, I cannot bring to bear any other protection for my books than my Lord Jesus Christ offered in respect of His teaching. When questioned before Annas about His teaching and receiving a blow from a servant, He said, 'If I have spoken evil, bear witness to the evil' (John 18.22, 23). If the Lord himself, who knew that he could not err, yet did not decline testimony against His teaching even from a most vile servant, how much more I, who am as refuse, and able to do nothing else but err, how much more ought I to demand and expect that nobody should want to bear witness against my teaching! Therefore I beg by the mercy of God that your most serene Majesty, most illustrious lordships, or any one at all, whether of high or low estate, who is competent, should bear witness, expose my errors, overthrow me by the writings of the prophets and evangelists. I am more than ready, if the case be proven, to renounce every error no matter what it is. I shall be the first to consign my books to the flames.

I hope I have made it quite clear by these remarks that I have sufficiently weighed and duly pondered the critical and decisive nature of my teaching and the dangers attached to it. I am well aware of the commotion and the dissensions it has stirred up throughout the world. I was duly warned about these yesterday in no uncertain terms. To see excitement and debate take place because of the study of the Word of God is to me plainly the happiest feature in the whole affair. This is always the pattern with the Word of God: this is the way it is, and this is the way it happens. Just as Christ said: 'I have not come to bring peace but a sword. For I came to set a man at variance against his father, and the daughter against her mother, and the daughter-in-law against her mother-in-law. And a man's foes shall be they of his own household' (Matt. 10.34–36). Therefore we ought to ponder deeply on how wonderful our God is in His counsels, yet how terrible. If we start by condemning the Word of God, then what began as an attempt to settle unrest would more likely degenerate into an intolerable deluge of evils. We must take every care that the reign of this most noble young man, Prince Charles (in whom, after God, we put all our hope), does not turn out unhappy and inauspicious. I could provide abundant instances of this from Scripture. For example, Pharaoh, the king of Babylon, and the kings of Israel. These men utterly destroyed themselves at the very time they studiously endeavoured to bring peace and settled government to their kingdoms by listening to the advice of the most wise men. It is God who takes the wise in their own craftiness (Job 5.13). It is **God who overturns mountains** before they know it (Job 9.5). Therefore it is God's commission that we fear Him. I do not say things with the implication that there is any need of my teaching or my warnings for men in such high office, but only because I do not want to withhold the allegiance I owe to my own land, Germany. With these words I commend myself to your Most Serene Majesty and to you, my lords, with the humble request that the passions of my enemies do not render me hateful in your sight, without just cause. I have no more to say.

When I had said these things, the Emperor's orator said, by way of reproach, that I had not answered the question. I ought never to have called into question those matters which had already been condemned or defined in Councils. What was required of me was a simple straightforward answer without horns (not an ambiguous, scholastic reply). Did I want to recant or not? (*This paragraph is actually in the first person*).

The Spalatin report is brief at this point and does not show the full force of von Eck's questions nor their penetration. We turn to the Aleander–von Eck report.

By rights, Luther, you have every reason to consider yourself favoured on all counts, for your case was presented to so clement an emperor, who listened to you for some considerable time with more moderation than you showed when you addressed him. Do you believe that this godliest of rulers heard with equanimity and ready ear all which you, with greater violence and more bitterness than becomes your religion or profession, launched against the supreme pontiff? Look at yourself! There is no moderation in you! See how propriety and modesty are utterly wanting in you!

Moreover, what about this deliberation of yours, which you were to declare to us? Namely, whether or not you wished to retract those books which you have acknowledged as your own, and to revoke their contents? You feel yourself circumscribed if you are compelled to revoke all of them at one and the same time and without distinction since not all of them are of the same substance nor of the same kind. You divide your books into three kinds. There are some in which you have handled matters of morals and faith so simply, sincerely and evangelically that even your enemies consider them harmless: in fact, even the apostolic bull, otherwise harsh and cruel, considers some of them inoffensive. If you were to revoke those books, you would be doing nothing other than condemning things which friends and enemies alike approve.

The second group is of the kind in which you inveigh against the Pope and papist affairs, as you call them. You revile their morals, their vices, their abuses, their tyranny and other things of that kind. You say that it is not right for you to revoke books of this kind lest you appear to strengthen their tyranny.

The third group consists of those books which you have written against those striving to defend the Roman tyranny and to overthrow your own godly doctrines. Here lies the source of all the dispute. If you were to revoke these, it would come about that the Roman tyranny would rule, under your patronage, more violently than it had ever ruled before.

Martin, you have not distinguished sufficiently clear between your dogmas and your books by these divisions. Those books you have published since the decree of the Supreme Pontiff are far more abominable and execrable than your earlier books, and they deserve to be condemned, inasmuch as they claim that the long-rejected heresies of John Huss are Catholic truths and at the same time undermine and weaken the whole authority and mystique of Councils. Furthermore, you have not answered my interrogations adequately by your statements. Let it be conceded that some of your books contain no harmful doctrine, a concession, however, we ourselves do not grant. Remove, then, the diseased and poisonous dogmas, remove the godlessness, remove the heresies and the approval of heresies, remove those things which damage the Catholic Faith: no harm will come from the wholesome things. His Holy Imperial Majesty will deal most mercifully with them if you change your views, and he will take care of the matter with the Supreme Pontiff that what is sound be not lost and abolished with what is unsound. If, however, you continue obstinately to persist in your notorious errors, and heresies, as you have begun, there is no doubt that all memory of you will be expunged from our midst, and that your writings, sound and unsound together will be condemned, and their author with them. And this is neither new nor unheard-of, for the books of the Arians and Montanists, of the Photinians, and likewise of the Nestorians and Eutychians and other heretics were burnt by the ancients though they contained much godly and Catholic religious thought. No doctrine is more effectively deceiving than that which mixes a few false teachings with the many that are true.

However, Martin, in the last resort you retreat and take refuge to the place where all heretics are wont to resort and have recourse. Of course, you say that you are prepared, since you are only a human being who is liable to slip and to fall, to accept intruction from the Holy Scriptures from anyone at all, from the highest to the lowest. However, up till the present moment nobody has been tempted to take you at your word, rightly so, as I see it. Is it not the case that all the heretics have always behaved in the same manner? Is it not the case that you, just as they did, want Holy Scripture to be understood by your whim and your own ideas? Is it not the case that you have appeared as the spokesman of mighty new heresies as well as those long since condemned? Many of the ideas you introduce are heresies of the Beghards, the Waldenses, the Poor Men of Lyons, of Wycliffe and Huss, and of others long since rejected by the synods. Is it right to open to question and to drag into dispute, those matters which the Catholic Church has judiciously settled, matters which have turned upon the usage, the rites and the observances which our fathers held with absolute faith, for which there was no punishment, no torment they would not have undergone, indeed they would rather have endured a thousand deaths than have deviated from them a hairsbreadth? Are you asking us to turn aside from the path which our fathers faithfully trod?

What will the Jews say when they hear these things? What will the Turks say, the Saracens and all those other sects opposed to our faith? How they will dissolve into laughter! What faces they will pull! We Christians are now about to discuss for the first time whether what we have believed up till now is right! Do not, I entreat you, Martin, do not arrogate to yourself that you, I repeat, that you are the one and only person who has knowledge of the Scriptures, who alone grasps the true sense of Holy Scripture. The most holy doctors, men who have toiled day and night in the exposition of the Scriptures, have attained this kind of knowledge with great labour and devotion. Do not make your judgment superior to that of so many of the most brilliant men. Do not seem to be wiser than all others. Do not cast doubt upon the most holy orthodox faith, which Christ, the perfect lawgiver, instituted. The apostles spread this faith throughout the world, miracles made it clearer, the martyrs confirmed it with their red blood. Later, holy doctors, discussing the obscure passages of the prophets and unveiling the greatest mysteries of the New and well as the Old Testaments, have disputed with heretics by sound argument and amply drawn out the faith. The deliberations of the sacred Councils have strengthened it. What the doctors have discussed as doctrine the Church has defined as its judgment. This is the faith in which our fathers and ancestors confidently died, and which they transmitted to us as our heritage. We are forbidden to argue about this faith by law of both pontiff and emperor. And since there is no end to arguing and disputing for many people, the censure of both pontiff and emperor is in store for those who rush headlong and in their rashness refuse to submit to the decision of the Church. Punishments are provided and have been promulgated.

For reasons of brevity, I deliberately pass over the rest of what you said, Martin, as not being appropriate to the matter in hand.

Therefore, Martin, it is no good your expecting a disputation on those matters, which you are bound to believe as certain and explicit *de fide*. Wherefore I think this same question must be insisted on time and again, and repeated, That you answer sincerely and candidly, not ambiguously and not with a logician's evasiveness, whether or not you wish to revoke and retract your books and the errors contained in them, and which have been disseminated by you. Yes or no! . . .

It is interesting that both accounts give the same verbatim reply of Luther. We return to the Spalatin report.

At this I gave my answer. (*The account is still in the first person.*)

Since then your Serene Majesty and your lordships require a simple answer, I will give you one without horns and without teeth, in these words. Unless I am convinced by the testimony of the Scriptures, or by evident reason, (for I put my faith neither in Pope nor Councils alone, since it is established that they have erred again and again and contradicted one another), I am bound by the scriptural evidence adduced by me, and my conscience is captive to the Word of God. I cannot, I will not recant anything, for it is neither safe nor

L

right to act against one's conscience. Here I stand! I can no
other!*
God help me. Amen.

The princes went into conference about the speech delivered
by Doctor Martin. When they had examined it, the official
orator of Trier began to tear it apart in this manner:

> Martin, you have answered more boldly than befits your person,
> and what is more, not to the point. You have made various
> distinctions in kind among your books, but in such a manner
> that it all adds up to nothing in relation to the enquiry in
> hand. If you had recanted those in which the greater part
> of your errors lies, no doubt His Imperial Majesty of his
> innate clemency would not have tolerated a hunting down of
> the remainder which are good. But now you resuscitate what
> was condemned at the General Council of Constance, a Council
> composed of the entire German nation, and want to be proved
> wrong on a basis of Scripture. You must be stark staring mad!
> What is the good of raising a fresh dispute on matters con-
> demned through so many centuries by Church and Council?
> Unless perhaps you take the view that a reason has to be
> offered for everything whatsoever to anybody who wants it.
> If it were once acknowledged that whoever contradicts
> Councils or the opinions of the Church has to be convinced by
> Scripture, there would be nothing left in Christianity which
> was certain or settled. It is for this very reason His Imperial
> Majesty seeks from you an answer simple and clear. He wants
> a no or a yes. Do you wish all your works to be regarded as
> Catholic? Or do you wish to retract any part of them?

Nonetheless Doctor Martin requested His Imperial Majesty not
to permit him to be compelled to recant against his own conscience, captive to be bound by the Holy Scriptures, without the
clear arguments of those who opposed him. If it was a matter of

*Last seven words inserted from earlier Wittenberg Account 1521.

an answer they sought, an answer that was nothing if not unambiguous, simple and straight, then he had already given them that. Unless his enemies could extricate his conscience by adequate arguments from those errors (as they call them) which hold it captive, he would never be able to free himself from the nets which entangled him. It cannot be maintained that whatever the Councils resolved is true for good and all. The Councils have erred and have often contradicted themselves. What is more, the argument of his enemies was not sound. He could not retract what Scripture unequivocally proclaimed. At this point he added the prayer, 'God help me!'

To these words there was no reply from the official except a few words to the effect that it could not be proved that a Council had erred. Martin assured him on the contrary that he was both able and willing to do just that. (*The Aleander-von Eck account reports some angry words of Eck, telling Martin to 'get rid of his conscience'.*)

However, since darkness had now fallen over the whole auditorium (on that account), every man left for his own home. As he stepped down from His Imperial Majesty and the tribunal a great crowd of Spaniards followed Luther, the man of God, with jeers, derisive gestures and much loud noise. (*The Aleander-von Eck report ends here.*)

On the sixth day after *Misericordias Domini* [19 April], when the princes, electors, dukes and the nobles of every rank who were wont to attend the assemblies had convened, the Emperor sent to the Diet this message, written in his own hand: 'Our ancestors, Christian princes in their own right, were without question, loyal to the Church of Rome which Doctor Luther now impugns. And because he is determined at heart not to move an inch from his errors, We for our part cannot move with propriety from the example of Our ancestors in defending the faith and coming to the help of the See of Rome. Martin himself, therefore, as well as his supporters, We shall prosecute with excommunication and in any other ways open to Us for their extermination.' Nevertheless, he was not willing to violate the agreement he had made and signed, and he undertook that Luther should return safely whence he had been summoned.

This pronouncement of Charles the princes, electors, dukes and imperial orders debated on the sixth day (19 April) throughout the whole of the afternoon, and even on the whole day, Saturday, which followed. During this time Luther received no communication whatever from His Imperial Majesty.

Here ends the report of the trial proper. For the proceedings after the trial the Aleander-von Eck report is silent. We depend again on the Spalatin report with supplementary information from the Vehus and Cochlaeus reports.

Further Proceedings after the Trial 19–26 April 1521

In the meantime [i.e. in the time between his trial and his departure] he was seen and visited by many princes, counts, barons, knights, nobles, priests, both religious and secular, to say nothing of the populace. These did nothing but besiege the house: they could not see enough. Two bill-posters were nailed up: the one against the Doctor, the other (so it seemed) for the Doctor.* Although the latter is thought by many of the well-informed to have been made by his enemies with malicious intent. The purpose behind it, they thought, was to make an excuse for breaking the safe-conduct, a situation which the Roman envoys assiduously sought.

On the second day after Jubilate [22 April], before breakfast, the Archbishop of Trier gave notice to Doctor Martin to the effect that on the fourth day [24 April] he was to appear before him at the sixth hour before lunch, at a place to be designated in the meantime. On the Feast of St George [23 April], after

---

* This placard was stamped with the *Bundschuh*, the tied shoe of the peasant, (distinct from the buckled shoe of the noble), a sign of his *tied* servitude. It was the dreaded symbol of peasant revolt, and was likely to do serious damage to Luther's cause. It would have been fatal to have been identified with social rebellion.

breakfast, the messenger returned from the court of the Archbishop of Trier at the command of the prince bishop, to say that Luther was to present himself on the next day, at the hour recently designated, at the lodging place of his lordship.

On the fourth day after Jubilate, the day after the Feast of St George [24 April], obedient to the command, Doctor Martin went to the lodging of the Archbishop of Trier. He was conducted there by the Archbishop's chaplain and the imperial herald. Accompanying him were those who had travelled to Worms with him from Saxony and Thuringia, as well as certain other highly trusted friends.* When he stood in the presence of the Archbishop,—with whom were Margrave Joachim von Brandenburg, Duke George of Saxony, the Bishop of Augsburg [Christopher von Stadion], the Bishop of Brandenburg [Jerome Scultetus], the master of the Teutonic Knights [Dietrich von Cleen], Count George of Wertheim, Doctor John Bock [ambassador of Strasbourg in Worms] and Doctor Peutinger [Secretary of the City of Augsburg],—Doctor Vehus, Chancellor of Baden, began to address Luther. He made it clear at the outset that Luther had not been called to this meeting to enter into controversy and disputation. It was only Christian charity and mercy that had motivated the princes to seek permission from His Imperial Majesty to exhort him in a kindly and fraternal manner. Next, on the subject of Councils, although they had maintained diverse views, they had never maintained contradictory ones. But even if they had erred greatly, it nevertheless still holds good that they did not destroy their authority thereby to such an extent that anyone should want to go against them and rely on his own interpretation. He made a reference to the centurion (Matt. 8.8) and to Zaccheus (Luke 19.6) and said a good deal about human institutions, ceremonies, and

---

* We know from other sources that Schurf, Amsdorf and Jonas took part. The evidence for the names of the the others is conflicting. Even Luther himself mistakenly wrote that Friedrichs von Thun was there, when in fact he was at a later meeting.

statutes. He maintained that all these things were sanctioned for the repression of vice in relation to the nature and problems of the time. He argued that the Church could not exist without human institutions. The tree is known by its fruit (Matt. 12.33). They say that many good things result from good laws. St Martin, St Nicholas and many other saints had taken part in Councils. He further stated that Luther's books would excite great disturbances and unbelievable commotion: the populace were using his book *The Freedom of a Christian Man* to throw off the yoke and to normalize civil disobedience. We have come a long way since believers were of one heart and one mind (Acts 4.32). That is why laws are necessary. Furthermore, it must be carefully considered that although Luther had written many fine things, and without doubt in a noble spirit, such as, for example, his *Of Threefold Justice,* and there are others, too, the Devil was working on this with his insidious machinations, so that in the end all his works would be condemned in perpetuity. For it would be by those he had written last he would be judged, just as a tree is known not by its flower but its fruit. Then Vehus added the reference to the destruction that wasteth at noonday, the pestilence that walketh in the darkness and the arrow that flieth by day (Psalm 91.5, 6). The whole speech was an exhortation full of rhetorical expressions about the usefulness and wholesomeness of laws, and again in turn, of the dangers both to the conscience and to the safety of the public as well as the private sector. Throughout his speech, at the outset, in the middle and at the end, he kept insisting on the same point, that this admonition came about as the result of the most gracious good-will and singular mercy of the princes. At the end of his speech he closed on a warning note. Looking to the future he said that if Luther were to persevere in his purpose, the Emperor would take proceedings against him and banish him from the Empire. He reminded Luther that he should think over these points as well as the others, and ponder them most searchingly.

The Vehus report goes into much further detail at this point.

He concedes the force of Luther's arguments, but courteously reminds Luther of his underestimation of the authority of the Church and the authority of conscience. The former has been expressed in the decrees of Councils, and though a scholar may find a deeper evangelical theology, he is not thereby released from that authority. These decrees may appear diverse but they are never contrary to the Gospel. The same applies to Catholic traditions and customs. It was an eloquent appeal to Luther to let well alone. In the matter of conscience Luther ought not to appeal to his own conscience against the views of all Christendom. Good men, Vehus argued, do not rely on their own opinion but humbly submit them to others. Luther is offended at the scandals of Christendom. Has he never considered the scandals that would arise from his teaching and the rebellion and unrest he is creating in society? Luther should consider the great loss to Christendom of his writings, for 'they have given fresh heart to men and exposed abuses in the Church': if he persists, these will be destroyed in their entirety. Luther's one course was to submit his writings to the Emperor and Estates, for them to consider, estimate and decide what to do.

In addition to these valid criticisms of Vehus, Cochlaeus adds still more valuable information and gives an account of the debate with Luther at this point not only on the authority of councils but on the divisive subject of the mass and transubstantiation, as well as communion in both kinds. It is of interest that this extensive discussion should have been reported by Cochlaeus alone, and would indicate the far-ranging and theological nature of these private proceedings.

We now return to the Spalatin report:

Doctor Martin answered:

Most clement and illustrious princes and lords, for that most clement and benign will from which this admonition proceeds, I tender my thanks as humbly as I can. I know that I am far too insignificant a man to be warned by such distinguished princes. Not all Councils were censured by me but only the Council of Constance, and that for the strongest reason of all, because it condemned the Word of God. This is clear in that it condemned the proposition of John Huss, 'The Church of God is the community of the elect'. This opinion the Council of Constance condemned, and in so doing condemned also this article of faith: I believe in the holy, Catholic Church.

He [Luther] did not refuse to pay the price with his life and blood, only that he be not reduced to the point where he might be forced to retract the clear Word of God. It is in defending this Word of God that we must obey God rather than man (Acts 5.29). Offences are of two kinds: the one concerns love, the other faith. Offences against love are in affairs of manners and life, but offences against faith or doctrine, which depend on the Word of God, cannot be avoided. It is not in his [Luther's] power that Christ should not be a stone of stumbling (Luke 2.34. Cf. also, Isaiah 8.14–15; Romans 9.32–33; I Peter 2.8). If faith were truly preached, and if magistrates were good men, the one law of the Gospel would suffice, and human laws would be rendered unnecessary. He knew that magistrates and the powers that be had to be obeyed, even if they were living evil and corrupt lives. He knew also that a man had not to yield to his private judgment: that was the very point he had made in his own writings. He only insisted that he be not driven into such a position as to deny the Word of God. In all other matters he would show himself as the most obedient of men.

When Martin had withdrawn the princes conferred on what they should order to be done with the man. Therefore, when he was recalled into the chamber, Doctor Vehus of Baden repeated what he had said earlier, and impressed upon Luther that he should submit his writings to the judgment of the Emperor and the Empire.

Doctor Martin took up the point humbly and modestly: he

did not allow nor would he ever allow it to be said that he had shrunk from the judgment of the Emperor, the princes and the Estates of the Empire. The dread of their judgment was so far removed from his mind that he would permit his works to be scrutinized in the minutest detail and with the sharpest criticism. There was only one condition. That it be done by the authority of Scripture and the divine Word. The Word of God was so clear to him that he was unable to yield, unless taught better by the Word of God. St Augustine wrote: He had learned to ascribe this honour of believing them true only to those books which are canonical, and that he believed the rest of the doctors, be their sanctity or doctrine ever so great, only in so far as they wrote truth.

St Paul had written to the same effect to the Thessalonians: Test everything, hold fast what is good (I Thess. 5.21) and to the Galatians: Even if an angel from heaven were to come and preach another doctrine, let him be accursed, he must not be believed (Gal. 1.8, 9). He (Luther) therefore besought them all the more not to violate his conscience, bound as it was by chains to Scripture and the Word of God, by forcing him to deny the plain Word of God; and that they would find him acceptable both in his private capacity as well as before His Imperial Majesty; and that he would behave in all points as their most obedient servant.

When he had said this the Margrave of Brandenburg, elector, asked him whether he had said he would not yield unless convinced by holy Scripture. Doctor Martin replied, Exactly, most clement lord, or by clear and evident reasons.

At this point the conference broke up. From this point to the end the report is to be found in Aleander's papers and is written by Johann Cochlaeus (1479–1552), an opponent of Luther and of the Reformation. Note the reappearance of von Eck.

While the rest of the princes were going off to attend the Diet, the Archbishop of Trier with his official Johann von Eck and Cochlaeus in attendance, summoned Doctor Martin into his

dining room. With Martin were Jerome Schurff and Amsdorf.*
The official began to argue like a casuist. He said that in almost
all cases heresies were born of Holy Scripture. For example,
Arianism from the text, The Father is greater than I (John
14.28). And again, from this passage of the Gospel, Joseph
did not know his wife, until she brought forth her first born son
(Matt. 1.25). Then he moved on from there in an attempt to
overthrow this proposition: the Catholic Church is the communion of saints. He even had the audacity to try and make
tares from wheat, and human limbs from dung. When he had
said these and such like things Doctor Martin and Doctor
Jerome censured him for playing the fool. Sometimes John
Cochlaeus interrupted noisily and tried to admonish Luther to
give up what he had already taken in hand, and for him not
even to teach any more. At last they departed. The Archbishop
of Trier was pleased to invite them to return after dinner. But
the official and Cochlaeus were not prepared to go as far as this.

After dinner Cochlaeus appproached Luther in his lodgings
with arguments which were utterly unacceptable. In this he was
restrained by Jerome Schurff, Justus Jonas and Tilemann
Conradi with temperate words. He had no hesitation in asking
Luther to abandon his safe conduct. He further exhorted him
to recant. Doctor Martin, to be sure, because of his incredibly
cultivated mind and his integrity, handled the man kindly.
He warned him as he was about to leave that he should not
yield excessively to his feelings. And further, that since he
intended to write against Luther he had better adduce the
authority of Divine Scripture. Otherwise, he would get nowhere.

*There is a very moving scene reported by Cochlaeus, an
incident that is illuminating to the discussion as well as to the
protagonists. The Count of Mansfeld, the patron of Luther's
boyhood, suggested that Luther and Cochlaeus should adjourn*

---

* Nicholas von Amsdorf (1483–1565) had journeyed with Luther from
Wittenberg to Worms. He had also been his companion at the Disputation
at Leipzig 1519. Jerome Schurff was his legal adviser.

privately to Luther's bedroom. Luther took a brother monk in case he needed protection, but in a tense and dramatic moment Cochlaeus assured Luther he was safe from any harm, for he was unarmed. Cochlaeus spoke appreciatively of what Luther had done.

Cochlaeus answered gently and sincerely: he had heard from the papal nuncio that all that was needed was the revocation of those articles manifestly against the Faith and the Christian Church; for the rest, a commission appointed by the Emperor and the princes would select the good from the bad in his books. In the event of his feeling fear or shame in the eyes of his supporters, the Emperor and the Archbishop of Trier would designate a quiet place where he could live in peace. He was young, strong and highly learned and he could still effect much good for others. He was now in the position where he could restore peace to the People of God by the recognition of his errors. Even if he were to have no regard for himself, he might have some for that godly genius, Philip Melanchthon, whom he was placing in great danger along with himself. At this point both men were on the verge of tears. . . .

Cochlaeus reminded Luther as a further point, that Luther could take heart in that the Pope, the Emperor and the princes were extraordinarily mildly disposed towards him. With regard to the matter of indulgences, he could not agree with him. Admittedly, Luther had been very vigilant in the matter of their abuse, but the indulgence need not on that account be abolished. . . .

And so they continued to converse, sincerely and from the heart, in Latin and in German. In the end Luther said, in German, My dear doctor, I well see that you do not deal with me with evil intent. I am the least in this affair. There are other, greater and cleverer. I preach and lecture publicly on the Psalms: I play a small role. Were I to recant loud and long, it would all be to no purpose, for other men far more learned would not keep silent but would carry the matter further. Full of emotion and bursting with tears, Cochlaeus offered to Luther a farewell handshake. Nevertheless, he said to him he would continue to write against him to the utmost of his powers, and fight for the Church. Luther reassured him that in that event he would get the answer he deserved.

The Vehus report at this point maintains that Luther was creating many difficulties with his writings. Vehus argues that a Diet is the wrong place to discuss these matters, and by its very nature could do little to forward the Word of God and evangelical truth, Luther's and everybody else's chief concern. Further, Luther was wrong to suggest that a Diet should be bound to the Word of God. The Catholic side was anxious that in the interests of truth Luther's writings should be entrusted to those who had no grievance against him, not to the establishment, nor to certain monks.

Vehus then expressed an appreciation of how much good had grown out of Luther's writings, all kinds of discussion yielding valuable developments and advantages. For example, the sophist theology and worthless preaching we have had hitherto, with their subtle Latin, worthless tags and epilogues and points, is an experience common to us all: he has ousted that and kindled the true spark of evangelical doctrine over a wide area. Similarly, his holding of the Word of God as being above men's opinions. The contrary has now got the upperhand. Human rules and commandments have been regarded and held as superior to the divine commandments, so that the Word of God has been thrown into the shade. Similarly, the excessive and arrogant activity of the indulgence preacher and his articles of enquiry, bringing the whole affair to the level of a town crier selling his wares. There is another point: the confusion in the heart of Roman life and practice. He admits to sketching it out rather extravagantly, but it has now got abroad, and he has stirred the hearts of many men to a finer view of these things. . . .

He had in his writings and teachings sought nothing but the glory of God, evangelical truth and the salvation of man. He could, therefore, with confidence entrust his writings to this Christian assembly to consider, weigh and estimate, and to abide by their decision.

After lunch they returned. They attempted again the same procedures as they adopted before lunch, but to no avail. They pleaded with him, as a concession, to submit his case to the judgment of a future Council. He agreed to this, but on the condition that they themselves would show to him the excerpts from his books which they were going to submit to a Council, and that they judge them by the testimony of Scripture and the divine word. Now when these men left Doctor Martin they reported back to the Archbishop of Trier that Luther had promised that he would submit some parts of his works to the judgment of a Council, and in the meantime would keep silent on the subject-matter of these doctrines. Actually Luther had never even contemplated this. Up till that time he had continued to refuse either to deny or to defame in any respect whatever that which pertained to the Word of God.

Therefore it came about by the work of God that the Archbishop of Trier summoned Martin to meet him in private. When he realized that the position was different from what the doctors had reported, he declared that the matter would never have been set right had he not heard him himself. Otherwise he would have gone to the Emperor immediately and told him what the doctors reported.

After all witnesses had first been dismissed, the Archbishop of Trier talked to Luther in the kindest way possible on the matter of submitting his works to the judgment both of the Emperor and the Empire, as well as to a Council. In the conversation which ensued Doctor Martin concealed nothing from the Archbishop of Trier, showing that he could not safely entrust so weighty a matter to men who approved the papal Bull, men who used new legislation and powers to attack and condemn the position of a man summoned under a safe conduct.

At that stage Luther's friend was admitted [Spalatin]. The

Archbishop of Trier then asked Doctor Martin to suggest remedies to meet this situation. Luther replied there were none better than Gamaliel suggested according to the testimony of St Luke, 'If this is the counsel of men, this work will be overthrown; if it is of God, you will never be able to overthrow it' (Acts 5.38–39). Let the Emperor and the imperial Estates tell that to the Roman Pontiff. For Luther himself was well aware that if his work were not from God, within three years, less, even two, it would perish of itself.

To the Archbishop of Trier who asked what he would do if articles were selected from his writings for the purpose of submitting them to a Council, Luther gave answer. He would agree, provided they did not select those points already condemned by the Council of Constance. The Archbishop of Trier said that he was afraid that they would be the very ones they would select. Whereupon Luther answered, 'About these I cannot and will not keep silence, for I am certain that it is the Word of God which is condemned by these decrees. I would rather lose my life and head than desert the crystal clear Word of God.'

When the Archbishop of Trier saw that Doctor Martin would never under any circumstances put the opinion of men above the Word of God, he very graciously dismissed him. When Luther asked the Archbishop to be responsible for obtaining for him His Imperial Majesty's gracious permission to leave, he replied that he would take care of that in a fit and proper manner, and inform Luther accordingly.

Not long afterwards* the official of Trier, attended by the Chancellor of Austria† and Maximilian,‡ imperial secretaries, visited Luther in his lodgings, and there read out to him the Imperial Mandate:

Because Luther has been warned countless times by the

---

* Actually a matter of a few hours, 3–6 hours according to various reports.

† Johann Schneitpeck.

‡ Maximilian von Sevenberghen.

Emperor, the electors, the princes and the estates, all to no purpose, but has shown the firm intent never to return to the bosom of the church and remain at one with her, it only remains for the Emperor as Defender of the Catholic Faith, to take proceedings against him. Therefore it is the Emperor's express command, that within twenty-one days from now, he return to the security of his own home under a safe conduct and in complete liberty, and that on the journey he does not stir up the people either by preaching or writing.

Luther, most Christian father that he is, replied most modestly and began to say:

As it has pleased the Lord, so has it happened. Blessed be the name of the Lord (Job 1.21).

First of all, to His Most Serene Imperial Majesty, to the prince Electors, to the princes, and to the sundry imperial Estates, I give most humble thanks for the kind and gracious audience they accorded me. And also for the safe conduct which they have honoured until now, and intend to honour to the end. I have wanted nothing in these proceedings except a reformation on the lines of Holy Scripture, an undertaking for which I have poured out so many entreaties. With this one exception I would suffer anything for His Imperial Majesty and for the Empire: life or death, fame or infamy. I would reserve to myself nothing at all save the liberty to confess and testify to the one and only Word of God. To His Imperial Majesty and to the whole Empire I commend myself most humbly, your most obedient servant.

Therefore on the next day, that is the sixth day after Jubilate (26 April), he bade farewell to his supporters and friends who had visited him so often, took breakfast, and then left at ten in the morning. He was accompanied by those who had travelled to Worms with him, and by Doctor Jerome Schurff, the jurist from Wittenberg. Caspar Sturm, the imperial herald, followed after a few hours, overtook him as he was leaving Oppenheim, and accompanied him by oral command of Emperor Charles.

And so may God preserve for a very long time to come for His One Church and His Word, this most godly of men, a man born to defend and to preach the Gospel. Amen.

5 The Verdict

The Emperor's Personal Statement

On the morning after Luther's second appearance, with a speed that took their breath away, the Emperor summoned the Electors and many princes, among whom Frederick the Wise was specially mentioned, to his presence at 8 a.m. He asked them what they were going to do now. They asked for time to think it all over. 'Very well,' said the Emperor, 'then first of all I shall show you what I intend to do.' He then read out to them the following document, written in his own handwriting. Aleander relates, with great satisfaction, that many of the princes went white as ghosts when they heard its contents. It was read out in French and then in German, and Charles sent it on to Rome, to be filed there.*

You know that I am a descendant of the most Christian Emperors of the great German people, of Catholic kings of Spain, of the Archdukes of Austria and the dukes of Burgundy. All of these, their whole life long, were faithful sons of the Roman Church. They were the defenders at all times of the Catholic Faith, its sacred ceremonies, decrees, and ordinances, and its holy rites, to the honour of God: they were at all times concerned for the propagation of the Faith and the salvation of souls. After their deaths they left, by natural law and heritage, these holy Catholic rites, for us to live by and die by, following their example. And so until now I have lived, by the grace of God, as a true follower of these our ancestors.

* Letters and Papers of Henry VIII. Vol 22. III. No. 6. RA. II. 594–6.

M

I am, therefore, resolved to maintain everything which these my forebears have established to the present, and especially that which my predecessors ordered, as much at the Council of Constance as at other Councils. It is certain that a single monk must err, if his opinion is contrary to that of all Christendom. According to his opinion the whole of Christendom has been in error for a thousand years, and is continuing still more so in that error in the present. To settle this matter I have resolved to stake upon this course my dominions and my possessions, my body and blood, my life and soul. It would be a great disgrace for me and for you, the noble and renowned German nation, appointed by peculiar privilege and singular pre-eminence to be the defenders and protectors of the Catholic Faith, as well as a perpetual stain upon ourselves and our posterity, if in this our day and generation, not only heresy but even the suspicion of heresy or the diminution of our Christian religion, were due to our negligence.

After the impudent reply which Luther gave yesterday [18 April] in the presence of us all, I now declare that I regret having delayed for so long the proceedings against the aforementioned Luther and his false doctrine. I have now resolved never again, under any circumstances, to hear him. He is to be escorted home immediately in accordance with the terms of the mandate, with due regard for the stipulations of his safe-conduct. He is not to preach or seduce the people with his evil doctrine and not to incite them to rebellion.

As I have said above, I am resolved to act and proceed against him as against a notorious heretic. I ask you to declare yourselves in this affair as good Christians, and to keep the promise you made to me.*

Written by my own hand, the 19th April 1521.

Charles

---

*On 19 February 1521. RA. II. 515, where the Estates promised to 'stand by and beside the Emperor' (*bei und neben bleiben*).

The Edict of Worms

The instrument of procedure was the Edict of Worms, a formidable document of some 30 pages, the essence of which is here distilled in the words of the original where possible. It is dated 8 May 1521, but was signed 26 May 1521 (RA II 640–659).

It pertains to our office of Roman Emperor to widen the bounds of the Holy Roman Empire, a task undertaken by our forefathers of the German nation for the defence of the Holy Roman and Catholic Church. This has been carried out by the grace of God and at a cost of much bloodshed, in the elimination and subjugation of unbelievers. It is also our responsibility, according to the rule hitherto observed by the Holy Roman Church to see that no stain of heresy or offence should contaminate our holy faith within the confines of the Roman Empire, or, if it has already caught hold, to extirpate it with due speed, appropriate means and with decision, as the situation demands. Therefore, we take the view, that if it was the duty of our ancestors to do this, much greater is the obligation to us. . . .

Certain heresies have sprung up in the German nation during these last three years, heresies which were truly condemned by the holy Councils and papal decrees with the consent of the whole Church. These have now been dragged out of Hell again. Were we to allow them to take root, and by our negligence to tolerate them and put up with them, our conscience would be greatly burdened, and the eternal glory of our name would be overshadowed with a dark cloud in the auspicious beginnings of our reign.

It is doubtless plain to all how far these errors and heresies depart from the Christian way, which a certain Martin Luther, of the Augustinian order, has been so bold to introduce into the Christian religion and its established order. He has besmirched these especially in the German nation, a people renowned as a tireless destroyer of all unbelief and heresy. He has sullied both our religion and order in such a way that

M*

unless it is speedily met the entire German nation, and after that all other nations because of its deep-rooted hold, will come to an inhuman division and a pitiable decay of good morals, a disruption of peace and Christian faith. . . .

The Emperor then describes the lengths to which the Pope and his advisers had gone to preserve the peace of Christendom. All these overtures had come to nought and it was his duty as the secular head of Christendom to impose their decisions as defined in the Bull.

After the delivery of the papal Bull and final condemnation of Luther, we proclaimed the Bull all over Germany, as well as in our Burgundian Netherlands, especially at Cologne, Trier, Mainz and Liège, and gave orders for its execution and implementation. Nevertheless, Martin Luther has not taken the slightest notice of it. He has not improved. He has not revoked his errors, nor sought absolution from the Pope, nor grace from the Holy Christian Church. On the contrary, he daily spreads abroad the product and results of his depraved mind and soul. He goes his way like Wodan's Wild Huntsman pursuing a public oppression of Holy Church. His weapon is his many books which are full, not only of new but of old heresies and blasphemies long ago condemned in sacred Councils. He spreads these abroad every day, in Latin and in German, written by him, or at least published under his name. In these books he destroys, overturns and abuses the number, the order and usage of the seven sacraments, held for so long by Holy Church, and in persuasive tones shamefully besmirches the unchangeable law of holy matrimony. He also says that Holy Unction is a fabrication of the mind. He wishes to drag our usage and benefits of the ineffable Holy Sacrament to the manner and practice of the condemned Bohemians. He now turns to attack Confession. This is the most valuable of remedies for hearts stained or burdened with sin. He argues that there is no basis to it and no profit from it. What is worse, he threatens to write further on the Confession to the extent that, if allowed, nobody would go to Confession, for they would be unable to understand his demented writings and would only say that confession is worthless. Further, some would preach that a man was not to go to confession.

He not only holds the priestly office and order in utter contempt, but even urges secular and lay people to wash their hands in the blood of priests. He describes the chief priest of our Christian Faith, the successor of St Peter and the true Vicar of Christ on earth, in scurrilous and shocking terms, and persecutes him with all kinds of unutterable polemics and invective. He further teaches that there is no free will and that all things are determined by immutable decree—a view he had adopted from the heathen poets.

He further writes that the mere reading of a mass on somebody else's behalf cannot bring them any nearer to God, but can benefit only him who properly fulfils it. In this connection he overthrows the customs of fastings and prayers established by Holy Church and maintained until this day. In particular he despises also the authority of the Church Fathers, an authority the Church accepts. He utterly takes away obedience and authority, and writes nothing which does not have the effect of promoting sedition, discord, war, murder, robbery and arson, and which does not subserve the complete collapse of the Christian faith. He teaches a loose, self-willed kind of life, without any kind of law, utterly brutish. He himself is a loose, self-willed person who condemns and suppresses all laws. This is shown when he burned in public the decretals and canon law, without fear and without shame. As he shows as much regard for the secular sword as he does for the Pope's excommunication and its penalties, so has he done greater harm to secular law and order.

He is not ashamed to speak publicly against holy Councils and to abuse and insult them as he thinks fit. In this context he has everywhere attacked bitterly the Council of Constance with his foul mouth, and calls it a synagogue of Satan, to the shame and disgrace of the whole Christian Church and the German nation. Those who took part in the Council and ordered John

Huss to be burnt for his heretical views, namely Our forefather Emperor Sigismund and the entire assembly including the princes of the Holy Roman Empire, he called the Antichrist, the devil's disciples, murderers and hypocrites. Consequently, all that was condemned by this Council in the matter of Hussite errors, he says is Christian and evangelical, and forbids its acceptance and observance. The articles which the Council approved and resolves he will in no way concede, and he has fallen into such a madness of spirit that he boasts that if the aforesaid Huss were a heretic, he is a heretic ten times over.

With that, all the other countless wickednesses of Luther must remain untold, for the sake of brevity. This one and only Luther is not a man but the Devil himself in the form of a man, under a monk's hood. He has collected a lot of heresies of the very worst heretics, long since buried, into one foul cesspool, together with some new ones conjured up by himself. He has done this under the pretext of preaching faith, an idea he inculcates with such industry as to destroy the true and genuine Faith. Under the name and pretext of evangelical doctrine, he has turned upside down and trodden underfoot all evangelical peace and love, the stability of all that is good, and the whole Christian pattern of life.

We have taken all this to heart. . . . On account of these affairs, we have summoned here to Worms the Electors, Princes and Estates of this our Holy Empire, and carefully examined on several occasions these very matters with great diligence, as the exceptional situation demanded. We have with one accord and one consent made the right decision, and conclude as follows:

Inasmuch as one so condemned and persisting in his stubborn perversity, a man sundered from the rites of the Christian Church, and a notorious heretic, is denied a hearing under any law, yet to avoid all unnecessary dispute, we summoned Luther to appear before us under safe conduct, simply to hear him, before we entered on further proceedings against him. We had another reason for taking this course: several people expressed the opinion publicly that many books written and printed in Luther's name ought never to have been written and published. For these reasons we summoned him to our court to come to us in company with our herald under the protection of a written safe-conduct, and, in our own presence, and in that of all the aforesaid as well as the Electors, Princes and Estates of the Empire, to give an answer in person to the following question: Whether he had written the books now laid before him and other books bearing his name. Whether he would revoke all that was written in these books against the sacred Councils, decrees, rites and customs held by our forefathers right down to the present day, and return to the bosom and unity of the Holy Church. This kind of thing was put to Luther, but they found his mind closed and harder to soften than a stone. And as soon as his books were enumerated he acknowledged them as his own, and further bore witness that he would never deny them. He added that he had also written many other books, to which no reference was made because we had no knowledge of them.

Charles then outlines the proceedings at Worms as well as the efforts of the subsequent commissions. All was unavailing for Luther would yield only to a General Council, but even then he would accept that only on the prior conditions that its findings were to be in accordance with Scripture. Charles, therefore, condemns Luther and gives him 21 days safe conduct.*

Charles then issues his orders against Luther and his

---

* It should be remembered of Charles that he was later to show again the same commendable magnanimity when he entered Wittenberg as victor in the Schmalkald War in 1547, one year after the death of Luther. He proceeded to Luther's grave in the Schlosskirche on whose door Luther had posted the 97 Theses 30 years before and whence all the trouble had begun. In a moving scene as he stood in reflective silence on Luther's grave, his companions in the flush of victory invaded his silence, with the suggestion that the corpse be exhumed and burnt. Charles instinctively recoiled and gave orders that the body be left in peace.

supporters and commands the destruction of all their writings.

We declare and make known that Martin Luther is to be regarded and considered by us, and by each and all of you, as a limb cut off from the Church of God, an obstinate schismatic, and a notorious heretic.

We, therefore, command each and all of you in this matter. We plead especially the obligation by which you are bound to us and to the Holy Roman Empire. We command your obedience lest you suffer the penalties of the crime of *laese majestatis,* and the ban and proscription of us and our Empire. This would involve the deprivation and the removal of all sovereign rights, fees, privileges and freedoms, which until now you have enjoyed from our forefathers and the Holy Empire in a unique way. We, therefore, by virtue of our imperial power give earnest expression to our will and command, that immediately after the expiration of the appointed 21 days, which terminate on the fourteenth day of the present month of May, you shall refuse to give the afore-mentioned Martin Luther hospitality, lodging, food or drink; neither shall any one, by word or deed, secretly or openly, help or support him in any way at all, nor help him with counsel and advice; but wherever and whenever you come across him or meet him, assuming you have sufficient strength to do so, you shall take him prisoner and send him to us in close custody; or you shall order that to be done; or, at the very least, immediately inform us and tell us where he might be captured; in the meantime, you shall hold him prisoner until you hear from us what further action should be taken against him according to law. And for such holy and pious good works, and for your trouble and expense, you will be properly indemnified according to law

Further, in the case of his confederates, supporters, patrons, promoters, sympathizers and their like, and of their property, personal and real, you shall, by virtue of the imperial constitution and of the ban and proscription of us and of the Empire, proceed in the following manner:

You shall crush them and imprison them, and take their property from them, put it to your own use, and retain it; and no one shall prevent your doing this, unless the victims show in good faith that they have abandoned their wicked ways and have secured papal absolution.

Further, we command you each and all, under the afore-mentioned penalties, that not one of you shall buy, sell, read, preserve, copy, print or cause to be printed, any of the writings of the afore-mentioned Martin Luther, condemned by our Holy Father the Pope, as stated above. This applies to all the writings and all other writings, in Latin, German or any other language, hitherto made by him, or to be written by him in the future. They are wicked, harmful and suspect, and published by a notorious, obstinate heretic. Neither shall anyone be so bold as to approve his opinions, nor hold them, preach them, nor protect them, nor assert them in any other way that human ingenuity can devise. All this notwithstanding the fact that he has introduced into them some good ideas, to deceive the innocent. . . .

I address each and everyone of you throughout our entire Holy Roman Empire and our inherited princedoms and lands, no matter what his status or position, but particularly those who hold authority and administer the law. To avoid the above-mentioned penalties you must destroy and blot out every single one of Luther's poisonous writings and books, referred to above. You must burn these books, and in this and in every other way, utterly do away with them. They serve only to create a great upset, and to produce damage, division and heresy in the Church of God. . . .

For the future no such wicked or poisonous books shall be composed, written, printed or illustrated, sold, bought or possessed, secretly or openly; they are not allowed to be printed, copied or illustrated in any way, nor in any other way yet to be devised; they are not to be concealed, nor are they to be procured. The Edict embraces under the description of wicked and poisonous books every kind of paper sheet, or copies of books, containing errors contrary to our Holy Faith and to that which Holy Church has hitherto held; also, polemical and abusive writings against our Holy Father the Pope, prelates, princes, universities and their faculties, or any other respected persons; anything that subverts from established virtues and the Holy Roman Church.

In the same way we earnestly command, on pain of the afore-mentioned punishments, all those ordained and appointed to maintain law and order, to tear up and commit publicly to the bonfire, all the writings, books, papers and pictures referred to above which have as yet been written, printed and painted, as well as those yet to be written, printed and painted (one manu-script adds 'including those written by hand'), no matter what kind they are or in what place they are found. This is to be done throughout the entire Holy Empire and our inherited lands, by virtue of this our command. Further, the writer, copier, printer and engraver, including the buyer and the seller, of such shock-ing writings, books, papers and paintings, who palpably per-sist after the publication of our present imperial command, will be proceeded against in the same way: Take his life, goods and perquisites where you can get them, imprison him, keep him in custody, and do with him as you think fit. You shall do this with good reason and within the framework of the law: you must do nothing against anybody, nor have anybody treated with more than or less than strict justice. . . .

We further decree that for the future no book-printer or anybody else, no matter who he may be or where he may be, in the Holy Roman Empire as well as in our inherited king-doms, princedoms and lands, shall print any books, or any other kind of writing in which anything is handled which touches upon the Christian Faith in greater or lesser degree. The first edition shall not be printed without the knowledge and approval of the ordinary of the place, or of his substitutes and deputies, with the approval of the faculty of Holy Scripture of the nearest university. Even other books (one manuscript adds 'sheets of paper and pictures'), no matter in what faculty they fall and no matter what the subject matter, are in no circumstances to be printed or sold except with the knowledge of the ordinary, nor efforts to be made to print or sell them. They are to be in no wise procured or permitted.

But if there is anyone, no matter his state, rank or character, who opposes in any way this Our Christian and imperial opinion, decree, statute, law, ordinance and command, which shall be held utterly inviolate ... such a man we shall bring to nought and render utterly powerless. We go further than that. Against such a person we shall take proceedings with the utmost rigour of the law, according to what we have written and according to the penalties of the law, and according to the form and nature of the papal ban and the imperial ban and proscription. ...

Mandate of Publication of the Edict of Worms*

26 May 1521, Worms

We, Charles V, offer to all authorities in our Empire and in our inherited lands addressed by this our imperial letter, grace from us and every blessing.

As an outcome of remarkable and stirring events, after consultation and with the approval of our imperial Electors, Princes and Estates, here assembled with us, We have issued an Edict and a letter of mandate concerning Martin Luther and a law relating to the printing of books, as you see herewith.

We therefore command each and all of you in this affair, under pain of the penalties, punishments and fines enumerated in the said Edict, letter of mandate and law, to treat this matter with the utmost graviy.

It is our will that this our Edict, our command, and our bans, be publicly proclaimed and studied by each and all of

*RA. II. 659–61. No. 93.

our subjects and yours, and those you have to rule and govern, and that they be commanded to avoid the aforementioned penalties, punishments and fines.

And that they be constrained to hold to this our imperial edict and command, obediently to live by it and comply with it in all points and articles. You yourselves must likewise obey. The expresses our complete mind and is our last word.

Luther's vindication of himself to the Emperor

When the decisive conferences permitted by the Emperor proved abortive, Luther asked for permission to leave. On Friday 26 April 1521 he left Worms taking the Mainz road north. Two wagons pulled out, escorted by 20 nobles. Luther knew that his destination was not to be Wittenberg though where else he could only imagine. Perhaps to a place of safety? Perhaps exile? Through Oppenheim, then Frankfurt (where he wrote a letter to Lucas Cranach which while courageous enough, yet showed some bitterness), and then on to Friedberg. At this point Luther sent back the imperial herald and wrote to the Emperor (WBr. 2. 401).

The importance of this letter is that it comes from Luther himself a mere three days after the trial. In it he seeks to explain his position and the grounds of his action. The reader can sense the exhaustion of the man, the uncertainty of his fate, whether he will ever get home to Wittenberg. Doggedly and tenaciously he makes clear the main points of his stand. The letter is of unique value as a confirmation of the official reports of the trial, with which it is in striking harmony It also has an arresting personal and emotional content. The letter further makes clear (what the author has sought to do in the text above), the importance of those official negotiations subsequent to the trial proper, when so much hung so delicately in the balance. Another striking feature of the letter is Luther's clarification of his views on the word of God which he here describes as the hinge round which the whole affair turned.

Luther to Charles V

Friedberg 28 April 1521

To the most serene and invincible Lord Charles V, elected Emperor of the Romans, Caesar Augustus, King of the Spains, of both Sicilies, and of Jerusalem etc., Archduke of Austria, Duke of Burgundy etc., my most gracious Lord.

There is a note written on the manuscript by Spalatin which runs: This document was not delivered to the Emperor, because in those difficult days no one could be found to deliver it for a long time.

JESUS

Most serene and invincible Emperor, and most gracious Lord, as your most obedient servant, I wish grace and peace to you in our Lord Jesus Christ.

When your Sacred Majesty granted me a safe-conduct and a free pass, and summoned me to Worms to find out what was in my mind in the matter of the books which I had published, I presented myself in all humility before Your Sacred Majesty and all the orders of the Empire, obedient to the letter of the law. First, Your Sacred Majesty ordered the question to be put to me, whether I acknowledged as mine certain books whose titles were read out; and, whether I wished to retract them, or was prepared to persist in them or not. For my part, I acknowledged at that point that they were mine (except insofar as my enemies may have changed something in them to its opposite meaning with some ingenious gloss or cunning trick). I indicated, with utter respect and humility, what my mind was in the matter. Namely: since I had based my books on clear and verifiable scriptural teaching, I could not yield to this request in any way: it was neither right nor proper to deny the Word of God and revoke my books. I humbly prayed that your

Sacred Majesty would in no way allow me to be driven to a revocation of this kind, but would rather take the responsibility for seeing that my books were examined either by you yourself, or by others of any rank whatever, or even by the lowliest if they were able, and the errors which they say are in them, be refuted by Holy Scripture, particularly by the Gospels and the Prophets. I proffered, with Christian promptitude, that if I were refuted and convicted of error, I would revoke everything: I would be the first to cast my books into the fire and to tread them underfoot They begged and prayed that I would give a simple and plain answer to all these questions: whether I was prepared to recant or not. For the second time I replied with all the humility of which I was capable: Since my conscience was held captive to the Word of God, the foundation of my books, it was impossible for me to revoke anything, until I was better instructed.

Then certain electors, princes, and other imperial orders negotiated with me to submit my books to Your Sacred Majesty and to the Imperial Orders for examination and judgment. Doctor Vehus, the chancellor of Baden, and Doctor Peutinger laboured to convince me of this course of action. I showed myself in the end as I was in the beginning: I would be corrected by Holy Scripture or evident reason.

In the end it was mooted that I should submit certain selected articles to the judgment of an Ecumenical Council and fall in with their decisions. As far as I am concerned, I was always ready in utter humility at any cost to do anything and to suffer anything of which I was capable. But my one most Christian concern I simply could not obtain, namely, that in my case the Word of God should remain free and unbound; and that were I to submit my books to your most Sacred Majesty and to the Imperial Orders or even entrust them to the judgment of an Ecumenical Council, it would be on the clear understanding that nothing contrary to the Gospel of God be submitted by me or defined by them.

The whole controversy hinged on this point. For God, who searches the heart, is my witness, that I am most ready to bow to and be obedient to Your Sacred Majesty, in life and in death, in glory or shame, in good times and in bad. I have often said, and now repeat, and make no exceptions to this avowal, apart from the Word of God, the Word of God, by which man not only lives, as Christ taught in Matthew 4.4, but which the angels desire to look into, 1 Peter 1.12; the Word which, since it is above all things, must be kept utterly free and absolutely unbound in all respects, as St Paul teaches, 2 Timothy 2.9. In no circumstances is it to subserve human opinion and to be imperilled, no matter how distinguished men may be in eminence, number, doctrine and sanctity. This is true to such an extent that Paul was bold to cry out and reiterate in Galatians 1.8, 'Though we or an angel from heaven were to preach another Gospel, let him be accursed.' And David says, 'Put not your trust in princes, in the sons of men, in whom there is no salvation' (Psalm 146.2f). Nor can any man trust himself to his own judgment, as Solomon says, Foolish is the man who trusteth in his own heart (Proverbs 28.27). And Jeremiah, Cursed is he who trusteth in man (Jeremiah 17.5).

In things material, which have nothing in common with the Word of God and eternal blessings, we ought to hold a mutual trust one to another. But the letting go of such things, when it is fitting to relinquish what has been kept, offers no danger or loss to our salvation. But in the matter of the Word of God and our eternal blessings, God does not suffer that to be brought into danger, which would happen if man submitted the Word of God to man's opinion. It is to Himself alone that God commands all men and all things to be submitted: He alone holds the splendour of truth, He alone is the truth itself. Every man is a liar and altogether vain, as Paul argues with such distinction in Romans 3.4. There is nothing wrong with that, for that kind of faith and submission is really that true worship and adoration of God which St Augustine teaches in his Enchiridion I, and which ought to be offered to no creature. For that reason St Paul considers that no angel, nor himself, and certainly none of the saints in heaven or on earth are worthy of this kind of faith which leads to worship. In fact he lays a curse upon such. The saints themselves would not tolerate it: they certainly would never seek it. Indeed, to trust in man in matters of eternal salvation is really to give the creature the glory owing to the Creator alone. For this reason I most humbly beseech Your Sacred Majesty not to regard this bias for the Word of God as born of an evil mistrust nor to interpret it ungraciously. It was born in me by what the Scriptures preached, to which every creature rightly yields. St Augustine said, that the authority of these scriptures transcends the total capacity of the human genius. I have shown my views and my faith sincerely to Your Sacred Majesty. Your Sacred Majesty will readily recognize from this that I duly appeared before you in complete obedience under your Sacred Majesty's safe conduct, nothing daunting, although I knew that my books had been burnt by my enemies and that in the meanwhile the Edict against me and my books under the name of Your Sacred Majesty had been publicly posted in many places. Such things would have terrified a poverty-stricken little monk like me and compelled him to turn back, except I had presumed on the Good God, as well also as Your Sacred Majesty and the Orders of the Empire, and I am still working on the same presumption.

Since, therefore, I could in no way achieve my end, namely a refutation of my books on a basis of Holy Scripture, I was compelled to leave without having received any answer. The whole controversy, as I have said, lay in this one point: they were not willing to refute by Holy Scripture those articles in my books which they considered erroneous; nor was any hope given or promise made that at any time in the future, an examination and trial of my books would be undertaken in relation to the Word of God.

Nevertheless, I offer my most humble thanks to Your Sacred

Majesty for having strictly upheld the terms of the safe-conduct, even at Worms, and for having promised to keep it until my safe return home. Finally, I beseech Your Sacred Majesty in the name of Christ, not to suffer me to be oppressed by my enemies, to suffer violence and to be condemned, since I have already shown myself so often as becomes a Christian and obedient man. I am more than ready, still trusting in Your Sacred Majesty, to stand before judges who are impartial, learned and free, secular as well as ecclesiastical, to be instructed by Your Sacred Majesty, by the Imperial Orders, by Councils, by doctors, or whoever else is able and willing. I am utterly ready to submit my books freely to everybody, to undergo and to accept examination and judgment. I make one single condition: they must be judged only by the Word of God, plain, clear and ever free. For the Word of God is deservedly higher than all else, and remains forever the judge of all men.

Wherefore, I pray and beseech you, not for my sake alone (for I am worth nothing) but in the interests of the whole Church, to allow the reasonable request of sending this letter back to Worms. From the depth of my heart I want most of all a mutual settlement by Your Sacred Majesty, the whole Empire, and the noble German nation, and it is my prayer that all of us may be happily preserved in the grace of God.

Hitherto I have sought naught else but the glory of God, the common salvation of all, nothing to my own advantage, never even considering whether my enemies would condemn me or not. And if Christ my Lord prayed for His enemies on the cross, how much the more ought I to pray for Your Sacred Majesty, for thy Empire and my own dearly beloved superiors and for the whole of Germany, my fatherland? I have the highest hopes in all of these.

I put my trust in this my explanation, and deeply moved with joy and faith in Christ, I feel bound to offer my prayer and petition. With these words I commend myself to Your Sacred Majesty under the shadow of the wings of our Lord God.

May He direct our salvation and keep us in His favour. Amen.
Written at Friedberg, Cantate Sunday (28 April) 1521
To Your Most Serene Majesty
Your most devoted suppliant
Martin Luther

Immediately on completion of the letter to Charles he wrote a similar though shorter letter to the Electors, Princes and Estates of the Empire (WBr 2. No. 402), dated likewise, Friedberg 28 April 1521. Luther was well aware how much of the affair, particularly the argumentation and justification, was beyond the linguistic and theological competence of the Princes, and yet how important it was to carry them along with him. Deliberately and patiently he worked his tired way through the main issues so that the Princes would have from his own hand some brief, authoritative statement of the debate. This letter adds nothing to what Luther has already expressed to Charles V, and is therefore not translated here. It shows traces of having been worked over by Spalatin.

Luther and his diminishing party hastened through Grünberg to Hersfeld where they arrived on 1 May. It would appear that Luther was anxious to do two things: to get into Saxony, his own territory, with all speed, and by the time he had reached his own country to have freed himself of most of his companions. At Hersfeld the abbot gave him a royal welcome and insisted that the tired Luther should have nothing else but his own bed. The abbot begged Luther to preach, and Luther addressed the Benedictine monks at five in the morning. This was against the express terms of the Emperor's safe conduct, but Luther took the view that the Emperor was acting ultra vires *in commanding control over a man's preaching.*

On 2 May he entered Eisenach, where the people begged him to preach and where also he wrote to his old patron of his schoolboy days, Count Albert of Mansfeld. The letter is a 1,500-word informal survey of the stirring events at Worms but adds no new information to what we have already given. It has a personal significance but is actually much less detailed even than the letter to the Princes and Electors.

Conclusion

The letter just mentioned was written from the picturesque little town of Eisenach, 'my own Eisenach', as Luther always called it, the town where he had grown up as a schoolboy and where he had known boyhood happiness to the full. On 3 May he drove through the majestic forests of Thuringia to Möhra, his father's early home, the place of his own people. By now he had shaken off all his fellow travellers, telling them he was to stay a little time with his own folk. Again they begged him to preach, and this he did in the open air, there being no church in the village. As he left those rough peasants and miners he was 'captured' by some friendly knights, who dispersed his companions and gruffly escorted the 'prisoner' at dead of night over the drawbridge behind the impregnable walls of the mountainous Wartburg Castle. There, still clutching his Hebrew Bible and Greek Testament, he was left to his own devices in the pseudonymity of a knight, 'Sir George' as the knights dubbed him, no doubt relishing the rough humour of their St George who had just slain the Babylonian Dragon!

From the tension and turmoil of Worms Luther was jettisoned into the serenity and solitude of an ethereal study perched high in the sky towering over the vast Thuringian Forest, the land which gave him birth, and for whose soil and people he had the German's patriotic affection. Within the space of eleven weeks he had translated into virtually perfect German the entire corpus of the New Testament—a monumental life's work for any other mortal.

But we must leave Luther sitting at this prodigious undertaking in 'the land of the birds' for our task ends here, save to suggest a few concluding reflections on the meaning of the trial for the sixteenth century, perhaps for the twentieth.

It was a tragedy for Christendom, recognized by most of Luther's contemporaries, and after four and a half centuries now widely admitted by Roman Catholic historians,* that the papacy lamentably failed to understand the Luther affair and scandalously mismanaged the whole Reformation movement. On the papal throne sat a de-theologized syphilitic, carried about by two male servants, in whose court crept a mass of crawling sycophants and secularized princes. Luther always groaned that God had never considered him worthy of a righteous and scholarly opponent with whom he could have reasoned a way through. Had the affair been in the scholarly and righteous hands of Cardinal Contarini, or of Cardinal Cajetan, or of the Archbishop of Trier or the Archbishop of Cologne, Europe would have experienced a reformed and revitalized Christendom, with possibly Luther on the papal throne and evangelical theologians for cardinals!

But as every historian knows facts have a propensity for being ugly: they were never uglier when Luther faced them in the sixteenth century. If the Reformation went the way it did by tearing Christendom in half, and then wracking the Protestant half with enthusiasm and liberalism, with socialism and politics, with schism and sect, and petrifying the Catholic half with its medievalism, we must recall that man's costliest error has always been to spurn fact and truth in his immediate self-interest: men do not gather grapes of thorns nor figs from thistles. If history is ever to make us wise it is perhaps man's failures that have to teach him most.

Let us sum up briefly Luther's concern. In the acid test of his own experience—the only valid authority which exists—Luther found that the monastic discipline brought him no nearer to God, and to no valid meaning of his own existence and way of life. He therefore questioned all that his contemporaries were saying of the term 'God', and their technique of finding God. He questioned contemporary theology: its doctrines of penance,

* e.g. Hubert Jedin, Joseph Lortz.

satisfaction, good works, absolution, indulgences, pilgrimages. He questioned all its accepted conventions of holy water, holy places, meritorious works. He questioned the whole doctrine of the Church, its priestliness, its secularized ecclesiasticism, its authoritative claim to infallibility and to be above Scripture, Council and sound scholarship. He questioned, and was to repudiate, the three 'heavenly ladders' of attaining the presence of God, namely, the ways of rationalism, mysticism and moralism. He questioned his contemporaries' certainty of God, their confidence in the church infallible with her long traditional techniques. God to him was unknown (*deus incognitus*), hidden (*deus abscondlitus*), appearing only in a contrary form—in humility, shame, persecution, in the despised Nazareths of the world, in the head that wore the crown of thorns not that which bore the triple tiara. The only God for Luther was the *deus revelatus,* the *deus incarnatus:* 'In Christ I have the Father's heart and will,' he cried. Luther's theology was his rediscovery of a biblical Christology: God found him in Christ.

When Luther was so converted all his personal problems were resolved. He now knew God and God knew him: he saw his whole life as in God's hands and under His direction. He then understood that this was the whole meaning of the Bible from Genesis to Revelation: it was the record, albeit human, of what God had done with those who had responded to Him, and of what He had said and made clear to these, His selected people. Here was the long record not of what man had been doing through the centuries, the valid and appropriate concern of the historian, but of what God had been doing and saying, the theologian's source material. To the Biblical corpus Luther applied his immense intellectual, linguistic and historical critical faculties. The Bible was the one single and central concern of Luther's life: what God had done with His people in history, and what He had said to their charismatic prophets. This is what Luther meant by the 'Word of God'. Not interpreted in any rigid, literal sense, but rather as a living Word which, when

N

understood in its historical context, because it is divine, is permanently and contemporaneously valid. The Word of God to Luther was always above Pope, Father, Tradition, Council, scholar: it was always subject never object, always judge never the judged. This is what Luther meant by being 'chained to the Word of God': he submitted his conscience and intellect to the work and word of God, and in free and open debate sought to submit the Church, her theology and practice, before the same bar, in the light of sound reason and historical and linguistic scholarship. With his theology straight, all the bad theology of his day, all the practices of penance, indulgences, pilgrimages, meritorious works, all the priestcraft with its threat of Hell and blandishment of Heaven, all the pomp of secularized clerics and infallible Popes, fell off overnight, like the old scab of a healed wound.

It was this kind of theology Professor Luther hopefully presented to the Church, and the tragedy of what we know as the Reformation was that responsible authority refused to listen and sought only to silence. All that Luther asked for was for competent authority to go into the malaise of Christendom, so that under God the whole Church, rebels and all, would together find the power to shake off the all too recent shackles of medievalism and the crippling weight of her own worldliness, and submit herself to the evidence of Scripture, to reason, to conscience, and to sound historical and linguistic evidence. He was simply a university professor counselling all men freely and collectively and soberly to look at the evidence and face up to conclusions.

Rome never answered Luther: she sought only to silence him and everybody who thought like him. True, stung to action she did rid herself within a generation of almost all the abuses which had shocked the world, but then the Reformation was not about abuses but about theology. True, stung to action she rolled back the forces of Protestantism to at least the northern half of Europe in the remarkable Counter Reformation. True, all the abuses have gone, and true it is that Roman Catholic scholarship is both reputable and acceptable in the fields of historical and dogmatic theology as well as in Biblical scholarship. True, also a new spirit of tolerance and understanding reigns in our churches and universities, and in society in general.

True as all this is, Europe (and the Christian world) fell into two camps: the Protestants who preferred truth to unity, and the Catholics who held the truth of unity and believed God would mend divided Christendom in time. The division is still with us. The author believes that on their own premises both are and were largely right, but that both need each other to be truly right. Protestantism cannot exist in its own right : Catholicism cannot prosper without it. Each 'side' has been dogged in history with its own nemesis, a sure sign that truth is impaired. Protestantism, on the one hand, has been dogged with a fissiparous sectarianism, a secularism which identifies its own good society with Christianity, a liberalism which runs out to an arid intellectualism, a lack of spirituality, the creeping paralysis of uncertainty and unbelief where even its theologians if not atheists are atheistic, a chilling radicalism, a disintegrating individualism, a laity which steadily drifts away on a better course.

Catholicism, on the other hand, though she has never lost her characteristic ethos, her spirituality, her sense of being the faithful scattered throughout the world, that sense in which a Catholic family is recognizable as such as easily in Chicago as on a country holiday, though she has never lost her charm and characteristics, she is, nevertheless, dogged by her own medievalism, ecclesiasticism and authoritarianism. Both are sick.

But God does not depend on his churches or his churchmen, for which we can all be relieved. He is active without them, all too often against them. Protestantism can be seen going through a searing, searching time, and where the churches are not moribund they are disturbed, restless and uncertain, crippled with uncertainty and unbelief, propping up old structures. Rome is similarly going through a world crisis of authority: priests and theologians are demanding intellectual and spiritual freedom; the laity are wresting power from the clergy; there is widespread questioning of dogma; there is universal criticism of church structures and the hierarchy; there is the alarming number of priests seeking laicisation; the outcry against celibacy and the unprecedented fact of priests openly living with women; the dismay over the Pope's recent decree *Humanae vitae* and the widespread disobedience; in Rome itself on Palm Sunday 1968 an educated Catholic layman stood up in the middle of the sermon to call the priest who was preaching 'a fool'. The signs of the times are unmistakable.

There is no doubt that a critical, objective, historical examination of Luther's trial and condemnation is a worthy and significant enquiry in itself. But over and around this study play a few subtle harmonics which it is well worth straining the ear to hear. First, there is the existentialist, contemporary tone that pervades the whole proceedings: the sense that it is we who are on trial as well as Luther, our institutions, our politics, our churches, our universities. And then, in a society which seems to drift, borne along by economic, cultural, social and political tides we can neither understand nor control—we drift into wars nobody wants, we are dictated to by economics nobody understands, we are carried along in a sea of pop art, pop music, pop urban development, pop universities which nobody questions —it is salutary to reflect on a man who would not drift but called a halt to the world with those memorable words, 'Here I stand!' And then there is that overtone, louder than them all, that Luther raised concerns that every theologian in the worldwide ecumenical debate must face squarely and answer truly, without fear of consequences, without fear of authority.

The questions that Luther raised, and which Rome never answered, are the very questions now gnawing her vitals—the authority of the Bible, the responsibility of individual judgment, the vast question of infallibility and the teaching office in matters of faith and morals, the freedom of the intellect and of historical enquiry.

Over and above its intrinsic value the trial of Luther might make both sides aware of what they are and why they are where they are. God does not give us men in every generation who say, 'Here I stand! I can no other!' He will give us another prophet in his own good time, but perhaps not before we have all seen the worth and significance of this one. And this duty is incumbent on all men, not only *homo religiosus,* for Luther belongs to our modern age, and perhaps more than any other man, begat it.

By any standards Worms was a singular victory for Luther, and meant a great theological achievement for religion as well as an immense political achievement for all men. Critics may say that already Luther's faults were manifest. They allege his intransigent theology, his individualism and obstinacy, his unawareness that this theology was leading society into social problems which he could not master. They allege his intolerance of the left-wing sectarian and socialist reformers with whom he disagreed, his insensitivity to the peasants. They say that he divided Christendom. All these charges may be answered, but not in this book. Suffice it to say that on the positive side he stands unequalled. There is his lion-hearted courage; his passion for truth and the consuming desire to communicate it in its naked splendour for all men to see; he was a religious genius; he was scholar, teacher, preacher; a master, rather the creator, of the German language. He was one of the few men history remembers for having taken a stand, and standing there against all comers till his death. Whatever friend or foe may say, Luther was the Reformation: he was the founder of Protestantism. It is the writer's hope that as men look back to the trial of Luther 450 years ago, they will not go back to him in history only but forward to him in thought. We have a long road to travel to catch up with him.

Bibliography

There are no readily available works devoted solely to Luther's trial and none at all in English. For general books about Luther, his theology and thought, and his place in the Reformation, the reader is referred to the following standard biographies, all of which contain full bibliographies :

James Atkinson, *Martin Luther and the Birth of Protestantism,* 1968

Roland Bainton, *Here I Stand,* 1955

Robert H. Fife, *The Revolt of Martin Luther,* 1957

James MacKinnon, *Luther and the Reformation,* 4 vols, 1925–30

E. Gordon Rupp, *Luther's Progress to the Diet of Worms,* 1951

Index

Abailard, Peter (1079–1142), 18
Accolti, 82
Acton, Lord, 9
Adelmann, Canon of Augsburg, 77
Albigensians (early reformers) 22
Aleander, Cardinal Girolamo (papal nuncio at court of Charles V) promulgates Bull, *Exsurge, domine* 1520, 91–2; promulgates Bull, *Decet Romanum* 1521, 96; speech for prosecution at Worms 115–130; demands on Frederick the Wise, 116; informs Curia of danger of Luther, 122–3; effects edict against Luther, 131, 139–40; absents himself from Luther's trial, 145
Alms, Almsgiving, 23, 24
Amsdorf, Nicholas (1483–1565), Colleague of Luther, 141, 144, 165, 170
Anselm, Saint. Archbishop of Canterbury (c 1033–c 1109), 18
Aquinas, St Thomas (c 1225–74) theology of, 18–19
Aristotle, 29–30
Physics, 29
Ethics, 30
Atkinson, James, 18n, 30n, 31n, 41n
Augustine of Hippo (354–430) nature of Augustinian theology, 18–19, 69; Augustine on faith, 191; Augustine on authority of Scripture, 192; *Enchiridion I*, 191

Augustine von Alveld. Franciscan Opponent of Luther, 93

Beier, Leonard accompanies Luther to Augsburg, 47
Bock, John. Ambassador of Strasbourg to Worms, 165
Brück, Chancellor of Saxony, 123
Bucer, Martin. Reformer of Strasbourg. 1491–1551. supports Luther at Augsburg 1518, 77; attempts to help Luther at Worms 1521, 141
Bulls
Unigenitus (1343), 49, 54; *Execrabilis* (1460), 54; *Exsurge, domine* 1520 – summary of text, 83–92; ineffectiveness of, 91, 154; mixed reception of, 92–3; burnt by Luther, 95
Decet Romanum 1521 – issue of, 90, 123; summary of text, 96–7; final condemnation and excommunication of Luther, 124
Humanae vitae 1969, 200

Cabot, 14
Cajetan, Thomas. Cardinal. (1469–1534)
Luther before Cajetan, 27; Pope consults Cajetan, 41, 43; examines Luther, 45–53; writes on

BIBLICAL REFERENCES

REFERENCES TO SOURCES